Love Letters of Jesus

"…LOVE believes the best of every person,
its hopes are fadeless under all circumstances,
and it endures everything…" - 1 Cor. 13:7

Misty Lea Chladek

WESTBOW
PRESS

A DIVISION OF THOMAS NELSON

Copyright © 2013 Misty Lea Chladek.

All rights reserved. No part of this book may be used or reproduced by
any means, graphic, electronic, or mechanical, including photocopying,
recording, taping or by any information storage retrieval system
without the written permission of the publisher except in the case
of brief quotations embodied in critical articles and reviews.

WestBow Press books may be ordered through booksellers or by contacting:

WestBow Press
A Division of Thomas Nelson
1663 Liberty Drive
Bloomington, IN 47403
www.westbowpress.com
1-(866) 928-1240

Because of the dynamic nature of the Internet, any web addresses or links
contained in this book may have changed since publication and may
no longer be valid. The views expressed in this work are solely those
of the author and do not necessarily reflect the views of the publisher,
and the publisher hereby disclaims any responsibility for them.

Any people depicted in stock imagery provided by Thinkstock are models,
and such images are being used for illustrative purposes only.

Certain stock imagery © Thinkstock.

ISBN: 978-1-4497-8433-1 (sc)
ISBN: 978-1-4497-8623-6 (e)

Library of Congress Control Number: 2013902293

Scripture taken from the Amplified Bible, Copyright © 1954, 1958, 1962,
1964, 1965, 1987 by The Lockman Foundation. Used by permission

Printed in the United States of America

WestBow Press rev. date: 2/26/2013

For my Lord –

I hardly have enough words to say Thank You. You have rescued me. You have given me life, a new life. Your timing is always perfect and the way you do everything always works. There is nothing impossible for you. You know every thought I have and even every hair I have on my head. You are so beautiful and glorious! You are the King of every King, your Kingdom is being revealed in the earth, and Your Kingdom will reign forever. Thank you for healing me, teaching me, drawing me to you. Thank you for your grace and your mercy. Thank you for giving me your love so that I may love you and know you. Thank you for being my Lord Jesus, my Father, my Savior, my King and my life. You are my best friend.

For my parents –

I'm so thankful God chose you two to be my parents here on this earth. I'm so grateful for all your patience and courage it took to walk with me through so many trials growing up. You both gave so much of yourselves to take care of me, to take care of us. Thank you for laying a Christian foundation in our home. I love you both and I am so grateful that we will be together always.

For my Disty –

Kristie, it is a privilege to be blessed with such an awesome sister. We are best friends, close and we have been since we were born. Thank you for giving of your life to help my life. You are a beautiful woman of God and joy just radiates from you. You are a wonderful teacher and your heart just pours out love on the children you encounter. *"Arise [from the depression and prostration in which circumstances have kept you—rise to a new life]! Shine (be radiant with the glory of the Lord), for your light has come, and the glory of the Lord has risen upon you!" Isaiah 60:1-3*

For my husband -

I'm so thankful God brought you in my life. I remember the day when looking at you I suddenly realized I felt as though I was "home." It was a knowing that we would be married and what a journey's it's been so far! Thank you for your love and patience and your constant encouragement each step. Thank you for being the loving groom God's called you to be. I feel His love every day with you and through you. I love you.

For all my dear friends and family who
have prayed and encouraged me –

Thank you for standing with me over the years and loving me with your words of encouragement and with your prayers. Be blessed.

"*__Wait and listen__, everyone who is thirsty!* **Come** *to the waters; and he who has no money, come, buy and eat! Yes,* **come**, *buy [priceless, spiritual] wine and milk without money and without price [simply for the self-surrender that accepts the blessing].*

Why do you spend your money for that which is not bread, and your earnings for what does not satisfy? Hearken diligently to Me, and eat what is good, and let your soul delight itself in fatness [the profuseness of spiritual joy].

Incline your ear [submit and consent to the divine will] and __come to Me__; hear, and __your soul will revive__; and I will make an everlasting covenant or league with you, even the sure mercy (kindness, goodwill, and compassion) promised to David."

Isaiah 55

....

For you say, I am rich; I have prospered and grown wealthy, and I am in need of nothing; and you do not realize and understand that you are wretched, pitiable, poor, blind and naked. [Hosea 12:8]

Therefore I counsel you to purchase from Me gold refined __and__ tested by fire, that you may be [truly] wealthy, and white clothes to clothe you and to keep the shame of your nudity from being seen, and salve to put on your eyes, that you may see.

Revelations 3:17 - 18

....

Ye are our epistle written in our hearts, known and read of all men

2 Corinthians 3:2

CONTENTS

FOREWORD

I can remember about the time that we first were getting to know Misty that she was in a serious struggle for her life.

There was a lot going on in her world, with doctor visits, family visits, and many just giving her support to stay strong.

One Sunday morning I can remember her making her way to the front of the church for prayer, with facemask on, and looking very tired. Like a soldier that has been in the battle.

As I was sitting in my seat, I heard the Lord say, "Go lay your hands on her, and proclaim that she would live to proclaim Gods goodness."

It is so incredibly awesome to see how God so sovereignly intervened in her life through the prayers and support of many.

Since those days, we have been blessed in seeing the miraculous transformation that she has been going through.

By the time, you finish reading this book, your spirit will be challenged and wrecked in God's incredible love.

Be forewarned that this book will change your focus before God forever.

As we read this book, God's presence snuck up on us and completely overwhelmed us with His love.

We pray that this book will bring you closer to Gods heart as it has ours.

Dwight and Anne Johnson

PREFACE

Many people I've met over the years who have heard about the miracles God has done in my life have said, "You're a walking miracle" or "You're a living miracle." Some have mentioned that writing a book would be a great idea so others would know what God has done. Yet every attempt I made was always met with mixed results. There were times I would sit down and begin to write and it began to look as though I was in a doctor's office and I was writing out a medical history from the past. It wasn't until recently that the pieces finally came together.

Many may ask why did I go through so much and I too even asked the Lord this at times. Just recently, God answered some very important questions that had remained in my heart. We are like His love letters to others. We *re*-present Him as He works through us. He loves so much that He desires for all to know His love and to know Him and have a very personal and real relationship with Him. On this journey, I'm given the opportunity to know Him, love Him and be known and loved by Him, to *re*-present Him and give the same love that He has filled me with. I'm not a special someone, no one popular or famous. We've all been given this same opportunity to know Him. This is the Good News! He restored it all, just because He loves You and because He wanted You to be with Him forever. When man sinned, he was separated from God and it would take God to make that relationship whole and complete.

We are like love letters of Jesus. When others see the things that I've gone through in my life since I was born and they hear the stories I pray that as they see they think on Him. He is so great! He is so good! May you see how He loves you and desires you to know Him and receive Him too.

His love is so great that He gave Jesus, the only begotten Son to be crucified in your place, a place that we all deserved to be. He loves us still. He desires us to be with Him still. His arms are still open wide.

This book began many years ago, about 17 to be exact. At the time, I heard the Lord tell me that I would write a book. Many of the miracles you will read about had not yet happened. Basically, it's out of obedience that I write this.

Many days I feel as though I am just beginning to know Him. It's as though my relationship with Him is just starting and my coming to know Him has just begun.

When I began asking the Lord again about writing this book, I was still asking him questions. I didn't know that there was a particular question still in my heart and I thought it had been dealt with long ago. I only knew the question was there when the Lord gave me the answer. That question was about the, "Why did I walk through this Lord." Earlier this year after listening to a message, I heard the words "Love Letters" and later as ministers began praying over our callings as believers that God has called us to, the Lord spoke to my heart very clearly, very loudly and it was, "You are my love letter." We are His love letters. We are living epistles that others read. We are to *re*-present Christ to others. He told me that it is because He loves me and because He loves you, and all the others that

He began me on this journey so that you would see Him and know Him too. He loves you so much!

The others contributing in this book are my parents, sister and dear friends of mine that my husband and I have become very close to and we are richly blessed getting to share Jesus together. All these have been a part of this journey with me, have seen the Lord working, and testify of His goodness and His love. Their contributions are vital to see a further picture of what the Lord has done and give Him praise for He is more than worthy!

"May blessing (praise, laudation, and eulogy) be to the God and Father of our Lord Jesus Christ (the Messiah) Who has blessed us in Christ with every spiritual (given by the Holy Spirit) blessing in the heavenly realm!

Even as [in His love] He chose us [actually picked us out for Himself as His own] in Christ before the foundation of the world, that we should be holy (consecrated and set apart for Him) and blameless in His sight, even above reproach, before Him in love.

For He foreordained us (destined us, planned in love for us) to be adopted (revealed) as His own children through Jesus Christ, in accordance with the purpose of His will [because it pleased Him and was His kind intent]"

Ephesians 1:3-5

Bless you and thank you,
Misty Lea Chladek

INTRODUCTION

This book is a brief account of the many miracles, some big and some small that God alone created in my life. I pray that as you read you will see Him and then know without any question God's faithfulness and His love no matter what circumstance we might be facing.

Having a very rocky beginning in my life with numerous health problems the Lord began to create miracles one after another. Doctors were not hopeful that I would live. My parents were far from a walk with God and didn't know how to trust Him, but would learn. I would experience desperate times crying out to Him, and yet believing that all things are possible with Him. Even when many others surrounding me were saying the opposite, the Lord said to stand, believe Him. Not just have faith, but have faith in Him period. Believe Him, everything He says. He is always faithful!

At a time when I believed God for a miracle and stood in faith, it seemed as though everything began to fall and I did not know what was happening, but God did. I would seek Him and ask Him continuously for a creative miracle, because I KNEW that He was able! Yet God's plans are so perfect! He did a creative miracle, but not as I had expected. Once I let go and just wanted His will and knew that no matter what

He did, I was His and it would be up to Him. I only wanted what He wanted. He created a miracle of a new life for me. In a way that stunned the doctors and left them puzzled with no answer but shaking their heads. I still remember the day that my doctor walked down the hall with me (he stands around 6'6" and I stand around 4'10", comical walking side by side) and he says, "Misty, do you know you're a miracle?"

You will also be reading about the supernatural encounters with the Lord that speak of His love and His mercy, like being saved in the desert when I had no direction and did not know which way to go. God provided a helper that took me the right way. Or when I was given the opportunity to visit a friend and share with her about what the Lord had done in my life. That opportunity almost felt lost when the time needed to reach her was not enough, but God made it enough by taking me there in a way that can only be described as supernatural.

I pray as you read you do see Him, see His love, see how He desires that we all come to Him and know Him. More than just being satisfied with those things that He can give us, He desires for us to desire Him alone. He created us to be with Him and He's just waiting for us to step aside from our busyness and begin.

ONE

UNCERTAIN BEGINNING

In 1970, a very happy couple, Chuck & Gracie, decided they wanted to get married and they did. On July 18, 1970, in a beautiful little chapel, they vowed to be together for better or worse, richer or poorer, etc. When my parents found out they were pregnant in 1971, they were elated. Doctors had told mom she could never get pregnant, so they knew this was a miracle in itself. Neither mom nor dad was very religious at the time. Mom had grown up going to a Methodist church and then primarily a Baptist church. Mom had given her life to the Lord when she was young, but her faith had grown cold. Dad had grown up going to a Methodist church with his parents, but didn't give his life to the Lord until he was 44. Despite their faith or lack thereof, they knew that it was God who created this opportunity to have a child.

Mom was told she was having a healthy baby boy. They prepared by getting one set of baby things and settled on painting the baby's room yellow instead of blue. Mom worked at her job up until her 9th month. She stayed very thin but she was very pregnant. In fact, her weight kept going up and this concerned the doctor who would in turn stayed on her case about not eating so much. As she tried to keep her weight gain down, she dreamt about eating potatoes any way you fix them. I suppose that was my doing, as I love to eat potatoes even today.

Not long before she gave birth, dad had a very significant but unusual dream. He dreamt that mom had given birth to a blonde haired, blue-eyed baby girl. He thought that was crazy, after all, they were having a boy. They had even picked out a name for him, Brandon Mitchell.

Mom was in labor for 72 hours. While in the hospital, in labor, the baby's heartbeat began to slow-down and the doctors feared the baby's life was in danger so, without hesitating mom was prepped and they performed an emergency C-section. When the doctor walked through the waiting room doors coming to see dad, he said there were two pretty girls he wanted him to see. Dad didn't understand. He said that his thoughts were, "Ok, I have a baby girl, and then who is the other girl?" Dad knew he wasn't allowed to see mom yet because of surgery. When he saw us, then his questions were answered. On April 8, 1972, two baby girls were born named Twin A & Twin B. Twin A was Kristie and I was Twin B. Together we weighed an ounce short of 9 lbs. I weighed in at 3 pounds 11 ounces, 16 inches long and Kristie was 5 pounds 4 ounces and 18 inches long.

Now that was a change of plans! Having a baby was a miracle but having two of them was an even greater miracle. When babies are born, one of the most important things to a parent is that child's health. In our case, one twin was very healthy and the other one was not. In fact, the prognosis that the doctors handed my parents concerning my health then was very negative. They had a few answers and wouldn't have all of them for a while. The doctors were unsure I would make it past 48 hours. They said "if" I made it past that mark, I might have a shot. Now for a couple that didn't know how to approach God or at least not in a long while, this was a desperate time. It would change their lives and they would learn to cling to the One who has answers, because so many would not.

There were prayer chains started all over and they continued through into my adult life. Can you imagine? So many people who I've never met have prayed for me. I've always wanted to say "Thank You!" God answered their prayers.

*"For You did form my inward parts; You did **knit** me **together** in my mother's womb."*

Psalm 139:12-14

"We are assured and know that [God being a partner in their labor] all things work together and are [fitting into a plan] for good to and for those who love God and are called according to [His] design and purpose.

For those whom He foreknew [of whom He was aware and loved beforehand], He also destined from the beginning [foreordaining them] to be molded into the image of His Son [and share inwardly His likeness], that He might become the firstborn among many brethren.

And those whom He thus foreordained, He also called; and those whom He called, He also justified (acquitted, made righteous, putting them into right standing with Himself). And those whom He justified, He also glorified [raising them to a heavenly dignity and condition or state of being].

What then shall we say to [all] this? If God is for us, who [can be] against us? [Who can be our foe, if God is on our side?]"

Romans 8:28-31

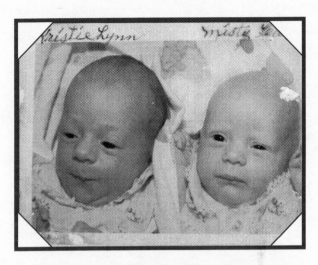

**One of Misty and Kristie's first photos
together at less than two weeks old.**

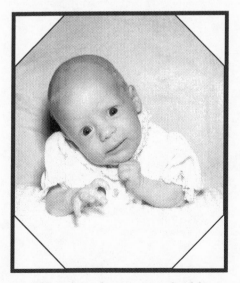

Misty less than a month old.

TWO

TAKING CARE OF THE BABIES

The first six weeks of my life, I stayed in the hospital in the preemie nursery. Mom would make it up to the hospital when she could, and dad would come see me after getting finished with work. I ate very little at first, and it took a long time for me to eat! I would take an ounce at a time and it would take an hour to feed me. While dad fed me, he would hold me with one hand from the top of my head to my bottom I fit in his hand. During that first six weeks, the doctors would learn a lot more about my health and they would again speak doubt over my life.

Mom and Kristie were released from the hospital at the same time and I'm thankful they had that bonding time together. There were so many, many times when the attention was always directed at me. There were so many critical moments, where the air just felt thick with questions and no answers. Sometimes when people are in their deepest need they reach out to God, but they do not realize that He's been waiting all along. I can almost picture my parents, even by themselves crying out to God. Maybe even wondering, did I do something that brought this? It wasn't anybody's fault. Many people look for fault when something bad happens because they want to make sense of the situation. Nevertheless, whether they knew it or not, faith began to build in them, believing that He was taking care of me. They had already seen Him bring me through the first two nights, and that was something tangible they could see. It encouraged them to have hope.

By the time I was 2 weeks old, the doctors discovered I was very anemic and decided I needed a transfusion. The decision was to use blood from my mom because they felt it had more antibodies that would still help me. After they shaved the hair off a small spot on the top of my scalp, they inserted an IV and gave me only 3 cc of blood. If you actually measure that out, it's something like a teaspoonful. Mom said I was so pink and rosy afterwards.

Next, the doctors discovered I had some issues around my heart. In checking my blood pressure one day, a nurse discovered different pressures on the left and right side of my body. In doing further testing, they discovered that I had pinches, like clamps in my aorta. Because the aorta being the main vein that runs to the heart, it became a very serious discovery. I was then introduced to a new doctor, a cardiologist. He was a good man, and he explained to my parents that he didn't feel I should try to undergo the surgery necessary to correct this until I was at least 4. They felt certain I would not be strong enough to handle it until that age, but how long of a wait that would be. The day I left the hospital the doctors expressed to my parents that they didn't expect me to live to be a year old. They told my parents to take me home and try to make me as comfortable as possible. I can tell you that my parents didn't take that message very well. I've been told my mother expressed to this doctor her thoughts about that, but more importantly she told him that her child would live. Because I live, it is proof that God has had other plans.

[11] For I know the thoughts and plans that I have for you, says the Lord, thoughts and plans for welfare and peace and not for evil, to give you hope in your final outcome."

Jeremiah 29:11

**Mom and dad bringing Misty home
and all of us being together.**

THREE

STEPPING INTO THE UNKNOWN WITH NEW DISCOVERIES

For those beginning weeks and months I was home, it was very trying. My parents told me of the many times they had to perform CPR because I was not breathing, or had to rush me to the hospital because I would develop complications and pneumonia. They had to watch me so closely. To this day when I see my mom the first thing she does is look my face over for changes. She doesn't tell me this, but I know. It may also be a bit of the reminder of how thankful she is. How thankful we all are today.

When I was about 3 or 4 months old, my mother took Kristie and me to see the pediatrician because I looked unusually pale. My doctor was such a wonderful and kind man. He did a quick hemoglobin count and found that my red blood count was dangerously low. Normal is 12 or higher and my count was somewhere between 4 and 5. I've come to understand that when the body drops as low as 7 it can put the body in danger of cardiac arrest. He simply said to my mom, "Now mama, we're going to just take this baby up to the hospital for some blood work." She knew something was truly wrong because this was a Saturday, and it isn't normal to do routine lab work on the weekend.

The pediatrician sent us up to the hospital to meet my first of many hematologists I have known. My mother had no idea what she might hear that day. The first thing the doctor told her was, "Well, she doesn't have leukemia." In a most shocked reaction, my mother responded with, "Well, I didn't think she did!" They did have to give me another transfusion that day, but she informed my parents that they would have to find out what was going on with me. They tried various treatments tried but to no avail. They tried B12 shots, which are used to treat pernicious anemia. They also tried folic acid and some other treatments as well. In order to give me the shots mom had to practice on an orange at home, because she had to give me these shots. Still, nothing was working.

It was in performing a bone marrow tap and sending those results to doctors across the nation that the conclusion was found to be the same. They concluded I had a rare blood disorder called Diamond Black-Fan Anemia. In fact, my doctor had the opportunity that year to meet Dr. Diamond, one of the two doctors that discovered this disorder, and this helped in that diagnosis. At the time, there had been 400 or less in the world diagnosed with this condition.

Having this anemia meant that the body didn't produce red blood cells on its own. There are only three options for a diagnosis like this. One is to be transfusion dependent for life and later undergo chelation to remove the excess iron accumulated in the body's organs from all the donated blood. The more transfusions a person receives, the harder it is to cross-match for a transfusion. Before someone can receive blood, his or her own blood has to be tested against blood that has been donated in order to get the closest match possible. This helps alleviate allergic reactions and problems. Some people who receive blood on a regular basis have a small list of regular donors, which helps with this cross match process as well as knowing from whom they receive blood.

The second option is to see if the patient will respond to steroid treatment. There really isn't any understanding of why some patients respond and some do not. As many people know, there can be many downfalls to steroid treatment for long periods of time. First, a patient with this type of anemia has an immune system that isn't working, as it needs to, and adding prednisone to the picture can compromise it even further making that person even more susceptible to sickness. There are many side effects of prednisone, but not everyone may experience them all. Thankfully, I did respond to this treatment. Many times when we would have to increase the dosage, the steroids would cause me to swell and have what they call "moon face", and my beautiful curly blonde hair then became straight. Our prayers were being answered having a treatment plan. Now during this time, things were moving fast yet they were slow. There were answers, yet there would be new questions all the time. Mom spent many countless hours poring over medical books learning how to ask the doctors just the right questions and to try to understand or make some sense of what was happening. She's become pretty direct with doctors over the years. I too have a no nonsense approach with doctors and talk directly with them. I want to know what they think, and I have had no problem telling them exactly what I think as well.

The other option for this diagnosis is to have a bone-marrow transplant. At the time I was born however, this was considered a last resort and not used unless there was no other option. Doctors have learned so much since that time, and I am so thankful.

Countless times, I was admitted in the hospital with

pneumonia. In fact, because I spent so much time in the hospital I was having a hard time learning to walk. Everytime I would begin to learn I would again go back in the hospital only to forget what I learned. My twin developed at a normal rate and stayed very healthy as she is today. However, from the time we were just babies she has always had a way of protecting me or looking out for me. One day while I was back to crawling again after coming home from the hospital, Kristie reverted to crawling too. As I struggled to learn how to walk, she would come along side me and hold my hand to keep me steady. Even then, she was helping me and she was so little too.

Kristie and Misty standing in the backyard at grandma and grandpa's house in Palestine, TX, holding a Cookie Monster puppet.

FOUR

This chapter was written by my twin sister to share her thankfulness and her testimony as a witness to God's faithfulness and love

KRISTIE'S LOVE LETTER

I don't remember a day going by that I didn't want to remove her suffering. I was always stronger, faster and got dirtier than she ever did! It was never fair, and even as a child I felt the sting of that indifference between us. As a child, she was the bravest person I knew. When we were little, I remember sitting together on the bench in the hospital hallways with her waiting for the lab to call us in. I would watch, as she would get her finger stuck for blood work. There was a reason the nurses always drew a smile on her Band-Aid or gave her finger puppets to put on her finger. We still put those finger puppets on our family Christmas tree.

I don't recall the day I understood that my sister was sick; I just knew she needed me in a special way, maybe more than most. I knew I would always try to be there for her, to protect her, maybe more than most. I remember thinking how I could grow up and become a doctor and then I could make her well. I wanted her strong and not sick. I wished she could run and roller-skate without wearing out so fast. When she got really sick at times, I wanted to not have to worry that she would stop breathing at night and not go check on her when I would hear her turn in her sleep. I wanted her to be well more than anything. It still wasn't fair. It wasn't fair for many years until the Lord healed her completely alongside a wonderful team of Doctors and nurses in San Antonio, TX.

In search for answers, I found one question that would just not leave my heart. As the writing of this love letter was ending, the Lord profoundly moved on my heart one afternoon to show me why He didn't heal Misty sooner. He first told me that He wanted her healed more than me.

This should not have come as a surprise but He showed me that every love letter written for her life had purpose and was for His glory. His purpose was so she would know His complete, unshakeable and unconditional love. Jesus was the bridge between glories and He alone carried her from glory to glory. The Lord used this time to establish His perfect love and Misty would know that His love alone would never fail.

I love Misty with all of my heart but this I know for sure, Jesus loves her more than my entire family put together does. The Lords ways are not our ways and His thoughts are not our thoughts. He just asks us to trust Him. He leaves the choice up to us.

From then until now she was the strongest witness for Jesus I ever knew and still know. I love you Disty!!

**Kristie and Misty spending time together
with mom and dad on their anniversary.**

FIVE

DISTY AND DISTY

My sister and I have always had a special bond. As we learned how to talk we developed our own language, which was interesting yet a frustration to my parents I'm sure. We called each other the same name of Disty because we couldn't say Kristie or Misty yet. One-day mom asked Kristie if I wanted something to drink and Kristie turned to me and gibbered something in our own language and then she answered mom. How weird! She and I don't talk in gibberish anymore, except when we start laughing, but we are still best friends.

Have you ever tried to recall a memory in detail? With eyes shut and getting quiet it is like waves as pictures begin rolling through your mind. Smells that almost seem like they come out of nowhere fill your senses and voices you may not have heard for years fill your ears. Then a movie begins to play and emotion fills your heart.

On a new spring day, sunshine filling the dining room and living room two little girls set out to play in the backyard. Misty and Kristie running around the yard, playing on the swing set. How high can you swing? Can I touch the sky? Let's play in the honeysuckle too. Have you ever tasted honeysuckle? It's wonderful and sweet! Don't mess with the bees!

A sweet memory I have is of honeysuckle. Having the windows open on spring days and early days of summer with the honeysuckle growing on the fence outside and the smell of honeysuckle wafting into the house and all in the backyard. Not every memory of those early years was made in a hospital or in doctor's offices.

However, every week and sometimes several times a week mom would take the two of us to the same hospital there in Ft. Worth, TX. I can still remember names and faces of those that took my blood work. They had to watch things so closely. It always seemed like it was the springtime or the fall we would see my hemoglobin change. This is also one of those memories that seemed to have smells and sounds attached. A number of people get anxious when they enter doctor's offices or visit hospitals. That isn't what I experience. Would it sound strange if I told you that there are familiar smells, familiar sights and sounds that put a person completely at ease? Smells of cleanliness are like that for me. When I walk into a hospital, it's almost as if I can smell the clean sheets and the linens when I walk in. Next are the sounds of the paging systems and seeing doctor's coats and nursing staff about their busy routines. Even with great doctors, looking out for my benefit there was only One that truly made me well and he gave wisdom to the doctors who saw me.

My parents had quite a challenge after bringing me home and trying to get in as normal a routine as possible while listening to all the different doctors' advices. The memories that were removed from my mind, I believe by the Lord, were the ones that involved the times of having pneumonia and going back into the hospital for lengthy stays or the memories of times when my parents had to do CPR on me to get me breathing again. These times were before I was 4. It's been explained to me that it was common for me to be in the hospital several times a year with pneumonia. Dad told me about what it would be like while I was there. He said that sometimes as we would be leaving for the hospital I would begin breathing better as they got me out in the night air. Something about the coolness of the air and the moisture that helps open the lungs to breathe better. While at the hospital, they would often place me inside a little tent that would stretch over my bed and inside would be very cool moist air that they would encapsulate me with and my body responded well to this.

There was such an occasion when we made a short trip to visit family in Oklahoma. We lived around Ft. Worth, Texas and it was a little bit of a drive but it was manageable. My mother's daddy had got sick with cancer and she wanted to see him. We made the trip there and by that nightfall, I had come down with pneumonia. It happened that fast. Mom tried to get them to admit me in the hospital there but they would not receive me because they were fearful of my medical past and that they would not be able to help me. Mom felt frantic and torn I'm sure, but she had to make quick decisions. She had to leave Kristie with her family there and she had to race me to the hospital in Ft. Worth as fast as she could. By the time I got there, I had gone into a coma. Mom and dad were able to get Kristie in a couple of weeks, but that was very unnerving. Dad was able to go to Oklahoma with mom the next time we tried to visit and again that evening I had developed pneumonia and dad drove as quickly as he could. Again, before we could arrive at the hospital I was in a coma. They did not try again to bring me that far away from home until I had undergone heart surgery.

The heart surgery took place when I was 4 years old and

they had worked hard to get me off as much prednisone as possible before they could begin. It went well and it has been well since that time. What a miracle though. At the time the surgery was performed, the ECHO Cardiogram was just a prototype machine and they had one in the basement of this hospital. They decided to try it out. They discovered areas around my heart that would have been missed had they not had this piece of equipment. I'm so thankful that was in place.

While in the hospital after the surgery, which I can still recollect those memories, the nurse kept trying to get me to eat but I really was not that interested. She tried offering me popsicles, gelatin, pudding, ice cream but nothing sounded good. She then asked, "Sweetie is there anything at all that I can get you", and I said, "Yes." I wanted fresh broccoli out of my doctor's garden. She looked at my mother and said, "Did she just say that?" My mother just laughed and said yes. The first thing I ate when I got home from the hospital was a big plate of broccoli and cheese my grandma had fixed me.

It didn't stop there though. Our very sweet neighbors called my room at the hospital and asked mom what they could bring that I'd like to eat and mom told her to bring me a can of beets. She asked if mom was sure about that and mom assured her, it was correct! I remember sitting up in my bed and eating that entire can of beets. I guess I really like vegetables.

"You will guard him and keep him in perfect and constant peace whose mind [both its inclination and its character] is stayed on You, because he commits himself to You, leans on You, and hopes confidently in You."

Isaiah 26:2-4

"I have told you these things, so that in Me you may have [perfect] peace and confidence. In the world you have tribulation and trials and distress and frustration; but be of good cheer [take courage; be confident, certain, undaunted]! For I have overcome the world. [I have deprived it of power to harm you and have conquered it for you.]"

John 16:32-33

Kristie and Misty spent a lot of time acting silly together.

SIX

COMING TO MEET JESUS

From the time I was little I had the desire to know God and felt Him close. I remember even before the age of 5 knowing of Him. I had always said prayers at bedtime usually with my parents. However, the year I turned 6 years old I gave my life to Jesus. My parents took us to a church where we would hear the Good News of Jesus Christ. However, there has never been a time when I did not think about Him or recognize that He is with me. I remember when I was little we went to the Baptist church near our house. I learned about Jesus in Sunday School and I learned about how God is His Father and that the Holy Spirit, Jesus and the Father make the Trinity. In my mind at the time, it did not understand how that works. However, I believed in Him.

One night after church while I was sitting at the table, eating a snack before bed and mom said I want you to hear something. She played a cassette tape for me and Kristie and it changed my life. It is called "The Love Letter". In this "letter", Jesus begins telling us how much he longs to be with us, to spend time with us and that He created the sunset and the sunrise just for us to enjoy. By the end of this love letter, I understood that Jesus wanted to spend time with me. He wanted to be with me. I remember saying those words out-loud. "He wants to be with me." The God of the universe wanted me to know Him. He was waiting for me to respond. He was waiting and I responded. My mama led me in prayer that night, I gave my heart to Jesus, asked Him to forgive me of my sins, and I meant it. I wanted to be with Him too. I now knew in my heart, that no matter what, I was His. It would be a number of years before I truly came to know Him more and more as my Lord, but He is my Lord and my Savior, and my joy. He is Joy.

Jesus,

Thank you for waiting for me. Thank you for wanting to be with me. Thank you for dying for me and I ask you to be my Savior. Please be Lord of my life. I want to spend time with you. Please be my best friend forever. I love you. Amen.

"If we [freely] admit that we have sinned and confess our sins, He is faithful and just (true to His own nature and promises) and will forgive our sins [dismiss our lawlessness] and [continuously] cleanse us from all unrighteousness [everything not in conformity to His will in purpose, thought, and action]."

1 John 1:9

I have always loved roses, especially the pink ones!

SEVEN

LEARNING TO TAKE A STAND

When I was 4 years old, my family went to visit a lake cabin in East Texas and we spent a handful of days there with my dad's parents. I first encountered something that was spiritual that weekend, not something good, but I was so young and my family was still ignorant of those kinds of things. It is possible that many people experience things when they are young, and not knowing what they encounter they don't know what to do as they have not learned yet. I remember waking up one morning there in the cabin and as I looked up at the ceiling, near the ceiling light, there I saw something that frightened me. Even before this time, my parents did not allow us to watch scary things on TV and I didn't have that kind of exposure, so it was not something that I dreamt. I was very much awake. It was very ugly, and looked fierce so without knowing what else to do I covered my head with the covers and called out for my mom. When she came in and I told her what I saw. She explained that I must have been dreaming. How could I explain to her what I had seen? This began years of needing nightlights, leaving a light on somewhere in my room and I can still remember staring at my ceiling light wondering about that day.

There were periods of time that I would be afraid at night and I would wake up with nightmares and then literally imagine snakes and spiders on the floor of my room, or my bed and I would bolt like lightening for my parent's room. I can still remember the feeling that if I could just get to my parent's room without hardly touching the floor that it would all be good when I got there. As soon as I got in their room either mom or dad woke up and for a long time my dad would come and pray with me and then I would fall asleep again.

This continued for quite a while. As I laid there I would sense fear and knew that it was not from the Lord, however until the Lord taught me different, I did not know what I was to do. One Sunday in church, I remember my pastor talking about fear. He said, "When fear comes in and you begin to feel afraid, you are to speak to fear and say, "In the name of Jesus, you must leave now! Go fear!" I can't describe to you how exciting that was! I wanted to jump straight up in my chair! I had the answer!! We have authority over the enemy in the name of Jesus! So, the next night I pulled my covers up near my face, really under my eyes and I again felt that same fear and I was reminded at that moment, what I was to do. Very quietly and directly I said, "In the name of Jesus fear you have to go now."

Immediately there was complete peace that filled my room, and I felt such relief and joy. I looked over to my right and I saw what I knew in my heart to be Jesus standing there in my room. I closed my eyes and I fell asleep. The next morning my parents who had not been wakened during the night by a young lady bolting into their room wondered what was different that night before and asked, "Misty, how did you sleep last night?" I always gave short answers, ever since I was tiny, and said, "Good." More probing from parents, "Misty, what was different last night compared to other nights. We didn't hear you or see you last night." I can recall the look on their faces today with open mouths. "Well, I did what the pastor told me to do. When I felt fear come in my room, I just said, 'In the name of Jesus you have to leave, go fear' and it left and Jesus was in my room with me last night and I went to sleep." Quiet was the response and "That's great Misty."

Jesus,

Thank you for protecting me. Thank you for teaching me. Please teach me all you want me to know.

"When you lie down, you shall not be afraid; yes, you shall lie down, and your sleep shall be sweet."

Proverbs 3:23-25

"For the weapons of our warfare are not physical [weapons of flesh and blood], but they are mighty before God for the overthrow and destruction of strongholds."

2 Corinthians 10:3-5

"That in (at) the name of Jesus every knee should (must) bow, in heaven and on earth and under the earth."

Philippians 2:9-11

EIGHT

THE CREATOR HAS MADE ME CREATIVE

From the time I was young I have been an artist. Mom and dad noticed I had an interest and they helped in that area by setting me up with art lessons when I was about 10 and I began developing those skills more. The desire to be artistic and creative is always a part of what I do. I know these gifts are from God and they are for Him. There have been seasons where there was space to be creative and times when there was not. There have been times when there was no resources to be creative, and there have been seasons when there was no real desire to do those things creatively because the desire was just "gone", however, when I think of Him, my heart dances. Those creative juices begin to flow and I start to picture in my mind new things and experiencing the Creator. The Creator gives us the desires to be creative.

Just like learning how to paint, it has been a progression to know Him. He puts the desire to know him and desire Him within us. If He did not put it there, it would not be. When we receive Him, it doesn't stop there. That is only the beginning. Even now, it is as if I am just beginning to know Him.

For from Him and through Him and to Him are all things. For all things originate with Him and come from Him; all things live through Him, and all things center in and tend to consummate and to end in Him.] To Him be glory forever! Amen (so be it).

Romans 11:36

Over the years, the doctors continued to watch me closely and it was a common thing to see my hemoglobin drop lower than it needed to be even on the prednisone, which happened ironically about twice a year, in the fall and in the spring, usually when allergies flared up. The way they dealt with this was by increasing the prednisone again. I used to despise this. It always meant that I would gain weight and especially in my face. As the hemoglobin came up within normal ranges they would start to taper the steroids and eventually the weight would come off, very slowly. My cardiologist also kept a watchful eye over things while I was growing up. He wanted to ensure that everything was growing as it should and all the scars where stiches were made grew at the same rate as I did so that there would be no complications. Mom told me that as I grew older the doctors continued to speak words of negativity or death over me and this was a constant issue that they refused to believe these negative words. She told me that when I was about 13 she finally told the doctors that she didn't want to hear it anymore. That the Lord had brought me thus far and it was up to Him.

It was because my cardiologist took X-rays once a year that he was able to show us the progression into my early teens and we saw a curvature in my spine. After many visits to the orthopedic, the decision was made that I would need a back brace. Some people undergo back surgery and receive implants to make their spine straight. The doctors and my parents were in agreement not to do this with me because I'd had heart surgery and they wanted to take no chances in complicating any previous surgeries. On December 23, 1985, at 12 years of age, I was put in a back brace that I had to wear for the next four years, 24/7 except for two hours a day, which usually included showering, sitting or swimming in the summer. I even had to sleep in it. I can still remember the day it was ready, just two days before Christmas. When I got it, I was horrified because the nice man who made it for me needed me to be in my underwear and bra with the brace over that in order for him to check all the fittings. I was so embarrassed and I did not want a man that I did not know looking at me half dressed! Recalling that moment, I can picture him on his knees next to me (I was and am short) and my mom sitting next to me, as I'm sobbing, explaining to me why he had to do this. The car ride home was filled with tears too. Because I was so shy when I was young and wherever we went, whether the mall or out in public I wanted my sister to walk in front of me. I could not stand for people to look at me.

This was a Milwaukee back brace. It came up under my chin and around the sides of my neck with metal and came up through my hair. It looked like I had two little ears sticking through my hair. It had a metal bar down the front with two metals bars down my back and it ended just below my backside. I hated having to wear this thing, even though I grew used to being in it. Every chance I got I hopped out of that thing! It also had these big screws on the front and on different areas so that when I wore my clothes over this these screws sometimes would rub holes in my clothes. Back then, my daddy was a design engineer and always thought of creative ways to do just about anything and he found a way to help me put the brace on using Velcro straps. To make it a little more interesting, I had to put it on without looking at it as it fastened behind my back.

I remember one day after school, I was hiding in my closet in the corner, crying. My mom found me there. I asked her, "Why did she want me? Why had they kept me? Wasn't I just a burden to them, a financial burden with so many health expenses and so forth?" She welled up with tears and told me no. That the Lord intended for me to be here, she was my mom, and she loved me. The Lord had purposes for me, and He had given me life. I just cried. I knew she was right, but I could not see that far yet.

Oh, the purposes He has for us. When we see just what is front of our faces, and just look at the circumstances, we might be facing now it can look very different from the whole picture. Remember:

"For I know the thoughts and plans that I have for you, says the Lord, thoughts and plans for welfare and peace and not for evil, to give you hope in your final outcome."

Jeremiah 29:11

At that time, this may be how my prayers would sound:

Jesus,

Please heal me. I don't fit in. I'm not like everyone else. I don't have many friends, but thank you for the ones you've given me. I want to be like you Jesus. I want to know you more. Please teach me your ways. Show me your ways and clean my heart. I give this pain to you. Thank you for loving me. Thank you for always being with me.

"I have strength for all things in Christ Who empowers me [I am ready for anything and equal to anything through Him Who infuses inner strength into me; I am self-sufficient in Christ's sufficiency]."
Philippians 4:13

Wearing the back brace in Oklahoma.

NINE

HE SPEAKS AND WE MUST RESPOND

In sixth grade, mom and dad took us out of the public school system and placed us into a very small Christian school. Every year we had a season of 12 weeks where we memorized scripture and had to quote it in front of a teacher where we received a grade for it. We memorized many scriptures during those years. Even today, I'm so glad we did that

When we finished eighth grade, Kristie and I attended a camp that summer that was related to the scripture memorizing we did. Every evening we had a sermon, music and then we would get to socialize with each other before we had to be in bed. Well, that one night, it is still as clear to me now as it was then. The sermon seemed so dry, and I could barely wait to get out of there to get a coke and something to eat and hang out with friends. I barely was paying attention to the sermon, when suddenly it was like there was a sentence that this man said that almost sounded like it was magnified in my ears. Although, I can't remember what he said, it is the next few moments that changed it though. I heard as clear as ever. "You gave your life to me. Remember? I want to spend time with you. I'm still waiting to spend time with you. Your life isn't your own. You gave me your life."

I remember looking behind my chair at the people behind me, beside me, all around me. Nobody seemed to have heard what I did. It was as clear as a bell. Believe me it wasn't because I was listening to this sermon either. I began to cry, and I could not stop. My sister came to see about me and asked, "Are you okay?" No, I wasn't and I didn't know what to tell her. I just kept crying and crying. My heart was so broken. I had let go of my time with Him. The Lord was speaking to me. Finally, a friend of ours that is extremely patient sat down with me, took me by the hands, and said, "Misty, its okay." I just told her it wasn't. She asked what was wrong. It's then that I told her what I heard while I was sitting there. I told her that no one else around me had heard what I heard, but I had not spent time with Him and He was telling me that. She just hugged me.

It is so interesting how the Lord knew who needed to ask me the right questions and to talk about the right things. She prayed with me and as we prayed together, I asked God to forgive me for letting go of our time together. It was so healing and it began a change in me that never stopped. From that point on, I wanted to be with Him all the time. I wanted to talk about Him, hear about Him, see Him, hear Him, and share Him. Anything that concerned Him I wanted. He put a passion in my heart for Him that just burned and it just grew. I prayed it would.

Lord,

I desire you. All I want is to be before you. I long to see your face, to walk hand in hand with you. You have put a fire and desire for you in my heart that just grows greater and greater. Thank you for your presence. Thank you for your Truth. Thank you for making me your child.

"I love those who love me, and those who seek me early and diligently shall find me."

Proverbs 8:16-18

TEN

HE IS CLOSE TO A BROKEN HEART

During the years of high school and college there were many times when I lost my focus on Jesus, but when I heard Him calling, I listened. There was this ever hunger and yearning for Him, although there were so many opportunities to look elsewhere and focus on other things, or things to get involved in. There was the Holy Spirit stirring my heart, reminding me to watch, to be careful.

In the dorm where I stayed in college, the girls there knew that I believed in the Lord. During those two years, I went through such a hard season. First, my dad's mom had passed away the fall of my senior year in high school and I still missed her. Then Grandpa got sick and even though I saw him over the Christmas holidays, I was too far to just take off and go visit. He was dealing with a brain tumor and he was terrified of getting an MRI. Without any exact diagnosis they could not operate. My parents and other family stayed with grandpa until he passed. I still remember the day my dad called to tell me. I heard the phone ring in the hall and I was visiting in my R.A.'s room. They looked at me and I told them I didn't want to answer it. I knew it was dad. They answered it, came, and got me. It was my daddy and I remember hearing him try to tell me that his dad was no longer here. It was gut wrenching to hear my daddy cry telling me his daddy was gone. My friends were very supportive, but there was this empty place in my heart and it burned deep. Nothing took this ache away. I hurt so badly. I missed my grandparents and didn't get to tell either one of them bye personally. My grades started failing as I missed more and more classes and all the umph went out of me at that time.

I remember driving to the outskirts of town to this place in the woods that I frequently visited to go pray, and I jumped out of my car and began to walk very quickly. I had visited that spot many times in the previous months just to get alone with the Lord, to talk. As I practically ran into the woods, I stopped in my tracks as I heard a growl in the distance and then suddenly running in front of me and stopping in their tracks were three small deer. The three just stood there just about two or three feet away and they watched me, and I watched them. Such a peace began to wash over me. That peace brought a focus and my thoughts were suddenly on the Lord. I cannot explain it. Just standing there, I was so reminded of my Lord and knew He was with me. He knew what I was going through and He would not leave me.

There have been many times in my life when I felt as though life was cratering in and the loneliness I felt was practically tangible. My Heavenly Father reminded me at that moment that I am not alone. He never leaves me. He will never forsake me. He will always love me and always be for me and not against me.

During the winter months that year, every time I longed for the Lord, or had that stirring in my heart I looked out the window, I asked Him for snow, and then I thanked Him for it! Every single time that winter, it never failed that within an hour or less after asking Him, I would look outside and it would be snowing. That winter they had records for snowfall. In fact, the night before I left to go to grandpa's funeral I asked for snow and it began and did not stop even into the next day, but I had to get to the airport. I asked the Lord to cease the snow so I could go, but to bring it when I returned. It began to cease and the day I returned there was a record snowfall that they had not experienced in years so much so that I almost didn't make it in that night. When the girls in the dorm would see it begin to snow, they would yell out down the hall, "Misty, quit praying!" I would just tell them, "No…, I will not stop."

Lord,

You are so wonderful! Thank you for hearing me. Thank you for revealing your wonders to others. Thank you for using me. I love you. Please open my eyes and ears to hear you, see you. I want to hear all you desire for me to hear. To know all you desire me to know. I desire you.

"You have not chosen Me, but I have chosen you and I have appointed you [I have planted you], that you might go and bear fruit and keep on bearing, and that your fruit may be lasting [that it may remain, abide], so that whatever you ask the Father in My Name [as presenting all that I AM], He may give it to you."

John 15:15-17

ELEVEN

HE IS THE GIFT GIVER

That year I had the most unusual birthday. That birthday in particular was my 20th and I thought my good friend had invited me to go with her to Phoenix for the day for a "birthday" surprise so I said sure. I thought, well, who knows, but I was excited to go. We drove from Prescott to Phoenix and traveled all day visiting car dealerships as she was getting quotes for her car to be fixed. It wasn't until around noon that I finally realized that she didn't know it was my birthday as we ate at a favorite Mexican restaurant that celebrates your birthday with fried ice cream and a free meal as they're way of saying, "Happy Birthday.". So, for the rest of the day I drove her to appointments and wherever else and by the end of the day I was tired, not to mention I felt a little out of sorts having spent my birthday so differently, and quite honestly I was feeling a little selfish, which also didn't help my attitude.

My friend and I had always been able to pray together and seek the Lord together. We'd never had any fights or major disagreements about anything. Well, that night as we headed back home, which should have taken about 3 hours, I prepared to take the usual route that I knew. She had a different idea. Her friends who had given her a place to park her car for the time being had told her a different route, which might save us some time. I didn't know this particular route and I was not comfortable, but after all I'd been through that day I just wanted to get home. As we traveled this road and the sun began to set, we began to see detour signs, one after another. After an hour or so on this road, and after numerous detour signs it had now become dark and there were no more signs. Not only was it dark, but we had also noticed that we were in the desert and there were no clues where we really were. Then ahead we saw a stop sign. As we approached we noticed there were no street signs, no streetlights and we had two options.

The road had come to a T and our choices were left or right. I had come to the end of the road and to the end of a slow burning fuse. I was mad. At this point, I had no more patience left and frustration began to build. I turned right, pulled off the road and began to let my friend know exactly how I felt. This of course was met with frustration that she was feeling and suddenly we were beginning to argue.

It was also about that moment that I suddenly saw this truck flying past my left hand side and pull off the road just in front of us. I had not seen headlights approaching and as dark as it was out there it didn't take much to see light over this open space of land, but nonetheless there it was. The man who stepped out of the truck was tall and had curly blonde hair. He walked towards my car. I knew with my headlights on there was no way he could see in because I had tinted windows and there was no light from behind my car to shine through. He walked toward my car right towards the middle and stood there. I'm sure my heart was racing as my hand reached for the door handle and gripped hard. There was no way I was opening that door. The man turned to my passenger side. Why? Would someone normally do that? He walked to that side and my friend rolled down the window.

The man bent down and looked straight at me and without hesitating he said, "You need to get on 'thus and such' road." I just looked at him dumfounded and not knowing what he meant. He didn't ask me any questions. In fact, he seemed to know exactly what I needed. He repeated exactly the same thing. Then he began to explain. You need to take "this" road and then take "that" road. I still didn't know what to say. My friend began to cry and tell this man that we were lost we were trying to get back home and where we were going. He never said anything to her. He looked at me again and he said, "Just follow me," and I said, "Okay." As he returned to his truck around to go back in the direction he came from, I turned mine behind his. My car was suddenly filled with an unbelievable peace. The Lord's presence just felt tangible. I knew at that moment who or what he was. I began to cry and all I could say was, "Jesus, you are so awesome. You are so awesome."

All the tension in the car was gone. I followed him down a road that I did not know the name of and before long, we reached another stop sign and another road, which took us to the freeway. This freeway led us back home. As we pulled up to the stop sign, he got out of the truck and walked to my side of the car. This time I rolled down the window and with tears still streaming down my face he said, "Is there anything else I can do for you?" All I could manage to say was, "You have blessed me more than you know." He said to take care and he got in his truck and drove away. I sat and watched his truck in front of me on the road, and then suddenly saw it no more. The ride home was interesting, very quiet, and very peaceful. As I finally got home, I learned that my friends at the dorm had been waiting all day to surprise me, but while on the way home, there was a reference of a scripture, Hebrews 13:2 that had been put on my heart, although I did not know what the scripture was until I looked it up. Before I did anything else, I went to my room, closed the door and opened my Bible. I looked up this verse and this is what it said, *"Be not forgetful to entertain strangers, for thereby some have entertained angels unawares"*

This was honestly the best birthday present I had ever had.

Jesus,

Thank you for the most amazing birthday present ever!! Your presence is truly tangible and your peace is perfect. Even when I fail, you don't. Even when my actions don't resemble you, you are consistent. You love me and take care of me every moment of every day. That was real Lord! Wow!! You are amazing... You love to amaze us with every sunset, with every color, with every breath. I love you and I praise you! Thank you for taking care of me and protecting me. Thank you for healing my heart and making me new.

**Misty sitting in grandma's rocking chair
that was recovered by her parents as
a surprise Christmas present.**

TWELVE

BEING MADE WHOLE AGAIN

The Lord can speak to us in so many ways and through the years, I've had many dreams in which the Lord revealed what he wanted me to know, sent a warning or gave me a direction in answer to a prayer. There are many accounts in the Bible of the Lord speaking through dreams.

One night as I slept I had a most unusual dream. I was standing in my grandparent's old home. There were people I did not know and some I did, including I saw my grandma there. She looked younger, strong and happy. She saw me in the kitchen as she was sitting at the table with others and she told me to come where she was. I began to cry standing next to her and told her I missed her. She just told me that she was doing great and it was okay. She said they had to go, but they were doing well and not to be sad, because it was good. Suddenly, after I walked outside I saw grandpa standing by their carport and he had a ball in his hand. He pitched it to my dad who was standing there. They were playing ball. Grandpa was then gone and I wondered where he went. He came back, he smiled and waved, and I told him I missed him. He told me that he loved me and not to worry. Then as I looked up I saw the most beautiful house in the sky, it was amazing. It looked like a large mansion. Then I awoke. There a peace surrounded me and I cried for quite a while. There was so much healing in my heart. What the Lord had brought was a gift. I was able to tell them goodbye for now. From that time forward things changed. I had no real way to explain what had happened, but I knew that there was peace and I knew that it was time to go forward.

Later after college, I met a friend who became closer than a friend and we decided we would get married. It was good at the beginning, but there were some who doubted that we were to be together and they worked really hard to try to pull us apart. During those years we were together, my health got bad. The new experimental medicine I was taking and the prednisone I took stopped working and even though I cried out to the Lord, it remained difficult. I began to learn about faith and how even though it was there in my life, I had never really understood what it was. God began to show me that my faith was to be in Him, period. Not what he could give me, but my faith was in who He was. Those were some tough years as I began to receive blood transfusions to keep me alive and I was hopeful and expecting creative miracles. It was during this time the Lord first put on my heart that I would write this book. At the time, I wasn't for sure what all it would contain, but I knew that before it was finished I would be well.

Those that desired for that marriage to end worked hard enough and I still remember that day as we cried together. He moved out, and then I did. It wasn't long afterwards that he filed for divorce. I was staying with my parents when I sought the Lord on what I should do. I was in earnest prayer one night and fell asleep. The next morning I heard very clearly to go, to go to Iowa. My twin sister lived there and I left that week for Iowa.

As I got to Iowa and began to be settled, I soon realized that some changes needed to happen. Besides needing income and still getting blood transfusions every 6 to 8 weeks, my heart still felt broken. Emotionally, I felt like a mess. My sister made a suggestion that began to grow in my heart. She suggested I go back to college. I remember praying specifically that if this is what the Lord desired me to do and where He desired I go that it would work out. Within a week, I was signed up and the next week I began. That was a miracle in itself.

When I first inquired at the school, I learned that they had adult dorms that only allowed those working on their master's degrees or those that were 25 or older to live there, and because I was 25, I knew I fit there. At the time I inquired, there were no rooms available and the classes I wanted to take were full. It sounded impossible. They put my name on a waiting list for the dorm and said they would call if something became available. I believe that was a week before school would begin and it was I believe on a Thursday. The following week I got a call. They had a room available and asked did I want it. You bet! I drove to the school and we figured out the classes and which direction I would begin. After finally getting my own room, there was finally a place to heal. After I would come home from class, I would shut my door and I would slide down the door onto the floor in a heap and weep. There was so much pain in my heart. Nothing seemed to change that except for just moments.

As I sat down in a chair one day and began to cry I suddenly remembered a verse a counselor had shared with me about six months before that. It is in Isaiah 55. It says, "The Lord God is your husband…" and just before remembering this I had cried out to the Lord and said, "It would be so nice to just hand some of these overwhelming things over to someone to help me." There were bills, paperwork and such. As the Lord reminded me of this verse, I lifted my hands in the air and said, "There, you can have it! I don't want this anymore. It is too much. You can have it all and I thank you for taking care of it all." He did. There was peace and this burden began to lift. For the first time in months, I was able to sleep through the night. That was my Lord.

He provided the food I needed and the financial assistance I needed. He provided the way. I was moving forward. I made friends, good friends; that really cared and were encouraging. Some of them just showed up and stayed by me, even when I didn't ask. It was so interesting that fall as I began to see winter, a real winter. I would have to make a conscious effort to listen to the radio for the weather reports for the day.

I remember one day in particular. I was getting ready for class and as I was putting on my makeup even with the radio going I quite clearly heard, "I have healed you. I have already healed you." I stopped what I was doing and looked ahead of me and repeated it and then recognized my Lord as speaking to me and declared, "Yes you have healed me." The next day again I began getting ready for class, in the same like manner and again while I was almost done I heard the same exact clear voice, "I have healed you already." Again, I agreed and declared verbally, "Yes Lord, you have healed me!" I became very aware at that moment while I looked at the clock and it was nearly 9:00 a.m. I knew that I needed to go to the clinic that day and have my lab work done. It had already been 5 or 6 weeks since the last transfusion and would have been time to prepare for another transfusion.

All these months much had changed so much of my time. I had been doing so much walking and it was good! At this point, I would walk across the whole campus and not be tired out and still had strength to spare. This was also the Lord. I remember my friend walking his bike while I walked with him across the whole campus. We talked all the way and when we got nearly to the dorms I suddenly realized I had not only walked to the other side of the campus without running out of breath, but also had talked and walked at the same time! I was so overjoyed I began to cry. This was a miracle!! Remembering these things, I knew I needed to find out what my hemoglobin was and what I needed to do.

After classes that day I went to the clinic, they did my blood work and I waited to see the doctor. He walked in, looked at me, asked me how I felt and I said, "Good." He said, "Well, you're fine you can go," and he began to leave the room. I almost grabbed the man as I stopped him and said, "Wait! What is my hemoglobin today?" He said, "Oh, why?" When I told him about all that was involved and why I needed to know, he said, "Well you are doing okay. You're hemoglobin is 11.9 today, almost normal."

I stood there in shock and my mouth open and began to cry right in front of the nurses. Joy, oh joy!!!!! Those poor nurses began to cry and didn't even know why they were crying. All I could say was, "Thank you Jesus, thank you Jesus." I told them and they cried more. You see, even when I received a transfusion normally it would only raise it from about an 8.0 to around 10.5 at best. I went home, called my mom, and said, "Mom I need to tell you something. Are you sitting down?" She said, "Should I be?" I said, "Yes." She said, "Before you tell me, I need to tell you something." She said that morning while she was at a Bible Study, the Lord had drawn her attention to a cross on the wall and she said, just as clear as day, the Lord spoke to her and said, "I have healed Misty. She is healed." She told me it was about 9:00 a.m. that morning and then I told her about my morning, and what time it was when I heard the Lord tell me I was healed.. When I told her about going to the clinic, she said she knew in her heart, as soon as I called that I would tell her that I was healed.

Jesus,

Words can't describe the joy I have! Thank you, thank you for setting me free! Thank you for loving me, healing me! Thank you!!!

"Now faith is the assurance (the confirmation, [a]the title deed) of the things [we] hope for, being the proof of things [we] do not see and the conviction of their reality [faith perceiving as real fact what is not revealed to the senses]."

Hebrews 11:1

But He was wounded for our transgressions, He was bruised for our guilt and iniquities; the chastisement [needful to obtain] peace and well-being for us was upon Him, and with the stripes [that wounded] Him we are healed and made whole.

Isaiah 53:4-6

Misty and daddy - Experiencing "moon face" while still taking lots of prednisone and still receiving transfusions.

THIRTEEN

A NEW WAY TO TRAVEL

After spending about a year at the university, there was a better direction it seemed. When I began in horticulture the first semester my thoughts were on how much I loved to garden. It wasn't until I took biochemistry or attempted to twice that I realized something was off. After meeting with my counselor, it became clearer. Did I want to learn how to grow a plant nursery or how to manage lawns on a golf course, he asked. No, not either of those things, but I did enjoy planting flowers and vegetables. I was told horticulture was not the direction to go. It was decided after a lot of time spent praying about it and searching and waiting, I would study photojournalism. I am just amazed when I think about how God brought so many neat people my way because of this.

God was doing so much in my heart and I was stronger than I'd ever remembered. I would talk to my hematologist in Shreveport on occasion. This doctor is a brother in Christ and someone that I consider a dear friend as well. He would ask me what I was doing different? I said, well I eat a little different, but overall I get a lot of exercise and things like that. He said, "Whatever it is that you're doing, keep doing that!" My hemoglobin continued to go up and I was so excited! I made a number of Christian friends there and I finally began to move forward.

In my second year there, I had rented my own apartment, and this was a first. It was different coming home and it was quiet. It took time adjusting, but it didn't take long. During those semesters, I was swamped with schoolwork and very little time for much else. However, as the semester was winding down before Christmas break there was a friend from back in Arkansas, where my parents lived, that the Lord starting putting on my heart. When I thought about her, I would just pray for her. Soon, when she came to my mind I knew that I needed to find her and share with her what the Lord has done. It had been a handful of years since we last talked and I had no idea if I could track her down.

Well, the Lord reminded me of her father's name and I looked that up and called his number. Sure enough, it was the right person! He gave me her number at work and I finally reached her. It was so good to hear her voice. I couldn't wait to tell her what the Lord had done and I knew that she would be so excited.

After getting to my parent's house for Christmas break, it was fun to unwind, but I had this nagging on my mind to meet with her as soon as I could. I called her and we set up a time to meet, on her lunch hour as it was the best time for me to see her. Well, she actually lived about 50 minutes to an hour from my parents and her lunch was an hour long, so in order for us to meet and have lunch and fit it in her schedule I had to leave my parent's house around 11:00 a.m.

That particular day seemed just like any other, and my mom had needed to go to the store for something and I stayed home to get ready. Well, in the need to do things a little easier, since my car was parked behind my mom's I gave her my keys to take my car to the store. It may have been long lines at the store, I don't remember, but all I knew was I watched the clock and realized that it was nearing 11:00 a.m. and mom was not back yet with my car. At this time, I didn't have a cell phone. This was actually, before it was the "normal" thing to have one. In fact, it was expensive to have one. Once I left to drive there, there was no way I could call her and ask if she was close or find out where she was. All I could do was wait. I watched it become 11:20, and then 11:30 and I began to feel anxious and a little upset. How was I possibly going to get there in time? Would my friend be through eating her lunch by the time I got there? Would she wait there anyway? Finally, I saw mom pull up and at this time, it was 11:40. A little rushed I said hello to mom took my keys and out the door, I went.

The route to get to my friend was simple. However, it took me 10 minutes from my parent's house to the edge of town just to get to the highway. On that highway, I knew I couldn't speed either, as I'd been stopped before and given a warning even when I was only 5 miles over the speed limit. I remember praying as I started out on that road. I reminded the Lord that He put her on my heart to see her. If He wanted me to meet up with her, He would make it happen. I remember continuing to watch the clock the entire trip. I saw every minute that passed on the clock.

As I traveled the road, it was beautiful that day, sunshine and blue skies. I looked up to see what I thought was a new water tower. I thought, hey, that's new, but as I passed it I read the words on the tower and it said French Port. Well, the last time I checked French Port was about halfway to my destination, but I'd only been on the road for about two minutes. I was thinking about this and realizing how peculiar this was and as I came around the curve, I suddenly was entering the town of my destination! What? The restaurant was inside the town, but suddenly there was my exit and I had to slow down because I would miss my turn if I didn't. I pulled in the driveway, looked at the clock, and could hardly believe my eyes. How did that happen? How did I make a 50-minute trip in 5 minutes? Lord? What? Not only was I not late, I was EARLY! I got out of the car and went inside and the woman asked me if I would like a seat. I thought, yes please. I sat down and waited for my friend to arrive. Yes, that's right. I waited for her because she was not even there yet and it was not yet 12:00. A very overwhelming knowing that this was a divine appointment came to my heart and mind. I knew that I was to be here and I knew that I was to share what the Lord had done. There was no doubt in my mind at all that the Lord had desired me to be there and He made sure I knew it. He made sure that I was there, and on time.

The Lord is amazing and all His ways are perfect. When I arrived back at mom and dad's house later I had to ask, "Did the road get shorter between these towns?" I then shared with them my experience and they were not sure what to think as I too was just blown away by the Lord.

It reminds me of the story about Philip and his encounter:

And the eunuch said to Philip, I beg of you, tell me about whom does the prophet say this, about himself or about someone else?

Then Philip opened his mouth, and beginning with this portion of Scripture he announced to him the glad tidings (Gospel) of Jesus and about Him.

And as they continued along on the way, they came to some water, and the eunuch exclaimed, See, [here is] water! What is to hinder my being baptized?

And Philip said, If you believe with all your heart [if you have [1]a conviction, full of joyful trust, that Jesus is the Messiah and accept Him as the Author of your salvation in the kingdom of God, giving

Him your obedience, then] you may. And he replied, I do believe that Jesus Christ is the Son of God.

And he ordered that the chariot be stopped; and both Philip and the eunuch went down into the water, and [Philip] baptized him.

And when they came up out of the water, the Spirit of the Lord [suddenly] caught away Philip; and the eunuch saw him no more, and he went on his way rejoicing.

But Philip was found at Azotus, and passing on he preached the good news (Gospel) to all the towns until he reached Caesarea.

Acts 8:34-40

"Behold, I am the Lord, the God of all flesh; is there anything too hard for Me?"

Jeremiah 32:26-28

FOURTEEN

CRYING OUT IN DESPERATE NEED

My health continued like this for the next two years. It was awesome. I had no more blood transfusions and I was even able to go on a mission's trip. The Lord had done so much! Things were good and yet there was a nagging desire that came up in my heart to be with someone. I was not sure about this, but knew that the Lord would show me. In time, I did meet someone. We had met on the internet. We came to know each other pretty well, I thought, and spent so much time talking and praying together. I felt very good about this and really had sought the Lord. I truly believed this was right. It really is important I believe that even if you meet someone online for it to be the initial meeting, but to really know someone you must spend time with that person. We didn't have that and I thought about that many, many times later. After spending many months getting to know him online, he came to visit and I had decided to move from Iowa to Texas.

It was different being in Texas this time though. This time I was not living in the area where I had grown up. This was San Antonio, very different from Fort Worth. After a while, I grew to know the area because I was also going to the University. I connected with a church there and this man that I was getting to know proposed to me. We felt so good about this and began making plans to get married. We still didn't have regular time together as he lived about two hours from there, although we tried to do counseling. However, no one was clear. Even though we did counseling people said things like, "Wow, this is going fast." I thought, "Yeah, it sure is, isn't that cool." It never occurred to me what they meant was this is too fast. However, it was like getting on a ride and not being able to get off.

There was a lot that began to change in my life. However, about a week before we got married I needed a transfusion, but the transfusions did not stop. They increased. I could no longer go to school as I was out of money and I began working, but could barely keep up with part-time work, as I was so tired. My body was experiencing so much at that time. Even after the wedding, it continued to get worse. He dealt with health issues too, and I found myself constantly trying to help him and take care of myself as well. There were times that it felt as though I was in a constant spiritual war.

The hematologist I met sat me down one day in his office and told me about what he saw when he looked at my lab work. Just like my first hematologist, he pulled up slides under a microscope in his office with my blood tests on them, and as he examined them himself he said, "Misty I see a lot of different red blood cells under here from a lot of people." I said, "I know." This was due to all the blood transfusions I'd received from different people by this point.

He talked to me about removing excess iron from my body as my body was overloaded and how bad that was. When you receive transfusions, you take on a lot of iron besides other outside sources like food. He also talked to me about different options. He asked me if I'd ever thought about a stem cell transplant or a bone marrow transplant and I said yes.

I told him that when I was 25 years old my sister and I had been tested to see whether we were a match. There was a doctor that checked this out during the time when my health had begun to change. At that time, the doctor had explained that we were a match, but had told me that I was just too old to get a transplant.

This new hematologist almost jumped out of his chair. He said, "That's it." He said, "I know this is not what you came to me to hear today, but this is what you need to do. Today I'm calling a friend of mine who is a transplant doctor and we are going to set you up with a transplant team and you are going to get a transplant." I sat there in shock and didn't know what to do. He got on the phone and called the doctor. He said we would be in touch as they talked things out, but in the meantime, he proceeded to continue in the same way we had with transfusions until further notice.

The desperation in my heart was enormous! I cried out to the Lord constantly. I trusted him with my very breath and knew beyond anything that NOTHING is impossible for Him. Someone during that time asked me if it was possible that the Lord would allow me to become sick again because of sin. I did not know how to answer that. All I know is that I cried out for Him, believed Him, trusted Him, and knew that without Him I had nothing and was nothing. He is my source. He is life. I asked Him continuously for a creative miracle, because I knew that was just like Him. I did not understand why this was happening and I kept asking the Lord this too.

My parents were in shock as they were not sure what to say. We had heard about transplantation over the years, however were told that if it didn't work that was it, you died. When I was younger, my parents did not want to do that. They were not ready to take that leap with so many unknowns. When I asked my spouse, at the time, about how he felt and or did this worry him. He began to cry and said he did not want me to lose my hair from the chemo. However, I didn't really care about my hair at that point.

In my seeking the Lord and trusting Him, there was one thing that I asked specifically for. I told the Lord I would go forward, I would walk wherever He took me because He was with me. What I asked of Him was to show me the end result. One night as I had my eyes closes and I was praying or just listening for the Lord, He showed me this picture. I saw myself whole, healed, strong and a new life. My heart was at peace and I went forward.

In God have I put my trust and confident reliance; I will not be afraid. What can man do to me?

Psalm 56:10-12

Behold, God, my salvation! I will trust and not be afraid, for the Lord God is my strength and song; yes, He has become my salvation.

Isaiah 12:1-3

FIFTEEN

MIRACLE AFTER MIRACLE

Not too long after this phone call, I met this transplant doctor. I call him the "tall one" and he calls me "shorty". He was shocked to meet me. He reminded me that this blood disorder was considered a "childhood disease" because most people with it didn't normally live to be this age. It was normally known only in children. He said he had been performing transplantation for about 25 years and he had been teaching others stem cell transplantation all over the world. He was one of the first to perform these new procedures. He had seen someone with this blood disorder years previously and the transplant he performed on that individual was not successful.

That did not sound encouraging. However, the Lord was and is with me. This was a new road, and the Lord was with me there. When I called my twin sister to tell her what was going to take place, it was very hard. She reminded me that I never had to ask her for a donation it was her privilege.

I'm so thankful. She traveled to San Antonio, went through more blood work and they began giving her doses of a particular medication which stimulated her stem cells. It causes them to travel from the marrow of the bone into the blood stream. After she underwent her last treatment, she was in a great deal of pain, but never told me. She had needles placed in both arms, we sat there together, and for six hours, we watched all the blood leave her body and return through the other needle back into her body. That was amazing to watch. As the blood left her body, it entered through a machine and in this machine, it was able to separate the stem cells from the rest of her blood and place it in a bag, like a blood donation bag.

That morning she asked them before we began what was the count that they looked for in order to do a donation. Before they could begin her donation, they took her blood work looking for a certain number in the stem cells and if it hadn't reached that number, they would not be able to do the donation yet. They told her if she was at a 12 or 15 (not sure what this measures against) she could donate. She asked, "What is the highest number you've ever seen?" They told her about 56 and when the doctor returned he told her that her count was 112. That was the largest they had ever seen. There was such a large donation that day that there was enough for two transplants and they would keep the other on hand and it would be good for another 9 years. When there is a donation done for transplantation, it is matched for just those two people and they can never give it to anyone else except the person it is being donated to at that time, no matter the size of the donation.

The doctors were just tickled that not only did we just match we had a "perfect" match. We were a 13 out of 13. They were looking for at least 7 out of 7. Her doctor which worked with her (as this is how they have to do this, the donor has a doctor and the recipient has a different doctor for legal purposes) told us that day how rare and special this really was because we had all of our major antigens matching and many of our minor ones too.

Kristie and I look nothing alike. However, our DNA doesn't say that! Three months later, we began to get ready. My doctor's first concern was the iron stores that were lingering in my body. The hematologist had already put me on an iron chelator called Deferral, which had to be taken subqutaneously. That means a little needle is inserted into fatty tissue of the body in order to give an injection. I had to have that inserted in my belly area, taped down as desferral ran thru a little pump through a tube and into me. I had this strapped to my body for 10 hours a day 7 days a week. There was no time for a break. As the iron would come off it would return immediately with the next transfusion. My transplant doctor had told us his plan for the transplant, which included a week's worth of chemo and one day of full body radiation. He explained that it would protect the body because the iron stores were so high and unless that level came down there was no other way to proceed.

There was a warning that went off in my head. I did not want to do radiation and felt that it was not going to go well. My parents felt exactly the same. We all began to pray and agree that the iron levels would come down. At that time, the iron levels needed to come down by over 3,000 points before we had the option of no radiation. You would have to look up what normal iron stores are to understand how truly high these numbers really were. Normal range is in the 100 to 200 range and my counts were over 4,000. That was deadly. When iron is too high it can saturate all the organs and cause them to stop working. There was NO OTHER WAY for the iron stores to come down to a reasonable level except the Lord because of getting transfusions so often.

I will not forget the day we sat in the room and my doctor

entered just shaking his head. My doctor was just baffled. He had run my counts that morning and that was the final run before we began the transplant. He said to me that morning he did not intend to run the counts again because he didn't want to receive a different reading, but he could hardly believe what he was seeing. That count had gone down about 3,000 points and I would not be taking radiation. Thank you Jesus! That was just another miracle that caused them to have no choice but to know and believe my God.

Lord,

I trust you and I thank you. I just desire you. You have already given me life and I receive it! You have blessed me with all things. Thank you for being everything to me, my strength, and my life. I trust you. I praise you…

I shall not die but **live, and shall** declare the works **and** recount the **i**llustrious acts of the Lord.

Psalm 118:16-18

Swinging on a porch swing at the Antique Rose Emporium before the transplant.

SIXTEEN

BY WAY OF FAITH

As we finally began chemo that week and they had me check into the hospital, it did not begin well. When they give such intense chemo, they have a normal procedure of giving anti-nausea medication to go with it. I had an adverse reaction to the anti-nausea medicine and when I recovered from that, we were able to begin again. This time they decided that they would not give me anything for nausea unless I needed it. There were three kinds of chemo that I was given.

We had all been praying and believing for no nausea and no bad side effects. Believing for no problems whatsoever with the chemo. To understand this better, that when you take chemo in this kind of quantity you are given papers to sign including signing a living will before you can proceed. They give you no guarantees. As far as you know that could be it. Chemo is poison. All your life you avoid poison. You know you would not want to intentionally take poison, and then suddenly you are agreeing to take something that could kill you. I was told that once I agreed to take it and it began there was no turning around. I couldn't then decide I didn't want to go through with the transplant, because this kind of chemo would wipe out my entire immune system and only in receiving the transplant would I then have another immune system. Wow!

I never got sick from it that week. In fact, I ate every meal. I did not lose my appetite at all. I remember looking at a bag on a pole with poison signs on it and watching it drip into a line that connected to my IV while I sat there eating my lunch and thinking, "Wow God...You are so awesome." The nurses are even so careful when dealing with chemo that they wear extra gowns, gloves and masks so they will not get any of it sprinkled on them. It did cause some strange things like dryness and an unbelievable thirst.

After I received the chemo, they never had to hook me up to an extra saline drip that week because I drank so much water! That also shocked them. That is almost never the case. So many little miracles happened, such as this, that the doctors had no explanation for them. My doctor had put me in the hospital because they did not know how I would tolerate the chemo. In fact, they were expecting the worst. Part of the concern stemmed all the way back from the beginning two weeks of my life in fact. Remember how I shared that the first transfusion I received was from my mom? Well, they don't ever do this anymore because they have learned that if anyone were to need a transplant from a family member and you have already received blood from your family member it can cut the chances of the transplant taking successfully by a large amount.

I remember my doctor coming in my room that week and sitting across from me and in his sarcastic humor says, "You're boring." I just laughed and said, "Great, I don't mind being boring!" I didn't mind being boring to them. Many came to see me off and on in the hospital. Unfortunately, I learned a lot of that later. The one thing I didn't like about chemo was how it acted with my memory. This is another reason they require you have a 24/7 caregiver before you accept having a transplant. There is no way you can take care of yourself, it is absolutely too much. The caregiver keeps up with the lists of medications, the appointments the procedures, and everything. About a week, before the transplant happened I had a transfusion and I remember telling my mom who was there, this is the last transfusion I will have to have. Well, my doctor was not so sure of that and he warned me not to be disappointed if I had to have blood while I was recovering and I told him I would not have to.

I had the transplant on a Tuesday morning, April 1, 2003. They gave me the transplant through a port in my chest called a central venous catheter. It helps nurses give you more than one medicine at a time if needed and it alleviates the need for countless poking and prodding with IVs. It was very painful and I had a lot of cramping and feelings of not being able to breathe, but they kept trying to assure me that it was from the alcohol that was in the preservatives that they had to use to store the donation. Yes, I admit and I apologized, but I was rude to my nurse. I asked her if she knew what the word no meant. I told her to stop because I was in pain and she said no. She couldn't. You see, once you have taken chemo they have no choice but to give you the transplant, otherwise it is just the countdown and watching the immune system you had die away.

For the next two weeks to three weeks was a countdown. During those three weeks, I would go home after being in the clinic every day and mostly sleep. At times, I could barely have conversations because of medications I was taking and because of exhaustion. The immune system goes through a phase where the white blood cells that were once living are dying and during that process, the body gets very weak. My body was so tired that I finally got to a point that I could no longer walk, but barely make it across the room. Mom had to return to work as she had not retired yet and I know that was very hard for her. My dad was my fulltime caregiver and the time that we spent together was such a blessing, such a bonding for a father and daughter.

He took such good care of me. They used to tease him at the clinic and say they wanted to clone him for all the others that needed caregivers. Some people never get to go through the transplants they need because they have no one there to help them. Can you imagine finding a match and a donor and they don't allow you to go through with it because there is no one there.

Every day was a routine of getting up early, going to the transplant outpatient clinic and getting lab work and waiting, and possibly getting fluids and maybe some magnesium by drip and then home again in the early afternoons. This was our routine. An interesting process that I learned in how chemo works as it is like setting a timer. The chemo I received attached to all the bad cells that were there and they affected only those. My doctor required me to stop chemo for one day and receive the transplant the following day. There was to be 24 hours from the last chemo treatment to the time in which I received the transplant. It is so interesting how the chemo does not affect the good cells, but only the bad cells and sets it on a "timer to die."

My white blood count (immune system) began dying and the new cells were waiting for the bad to go. On the day that the doctor did my lab work and came back to tell us that we were finally at zero, was an anticipated day. It meant that I had no immune system at all. So many precautions had been taken everywhere I went. I wore masks everywhere. People would stare and wonder what was going on with this woman who was wearing hats, had no hair, had tubes sticking up through her shirt and wearing a mask on her face. It was not a pleasure going out in public, although I didn't get to do that very much anyway. They had many rules for me to follow to help protect me from coming into contact with germs and diseases.

I could not play with dirt because it has organisms that they said would harm me. I had a special diet and could not eat fresh fruits except those with thick skins and everything was cooked very well as to avoid contamination. I could not have cheese or other things that were favorites. The day after the news of the white blood cell count dropping to zero, we came expecting good news. You see, the goal is that as soon as zero hits on the white blood cells that the transplant will begin to grow and the numbers will begin again and this time it is the good stuff! That day was to celebrate. This was the goal. That day, around 24 hours after the first news of it finally arriving at zero, the doctor walked in and said, "Now Misty I don't want you to get too excited about this just yet, but your count is 1.0 and your red blood cells also seem to be going up too. Tears… joy…. indescribable…. We had other news that day too.

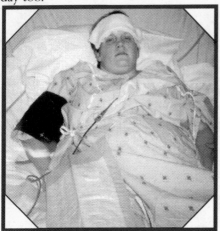

Receiving the transplant.

And He said to her, Daughter, your faith (your trust and confidence in Me, springing from faith in God) has restored you to health. Go in (into) peace and be continually healed and freed from your [distressing bodily] disease.

Mark 5:33-35

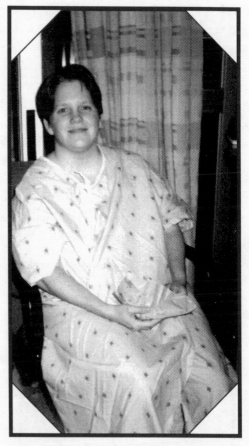

**Following the transplant and feeling
better after the medication.**

SEVENTEEN

ALL HIS WAYS ARE PERFECT

"But now [in spite of past judgments for Israel's sins], thus says the Lord, He Who created you, O Jacob, and He Who formed you, O Israel: Fear not, for I have redeemed you [ransomed you by paying a price instead of leaving you captives]; I have called you by your name; you are Mine.

When you pass through the waters, I will be with you, and through the rivers, they will not overwhelm you. When you walk through the fire, you will not be burned or scorched, nor will the flame kindle upon you."

Isaiah 43:1-2

Every day mom and I would talk and she would pray this verse with me and we would speak it aloud together.

Mom and dad had been praying that the Lord would make a way for me to be in the hospital during this time while my immune system was still almost nothing. They felt by me being in the hospital during this time, would be the only true way for me to get the rest I needed and safety from anything that would cause me harm. That day after our news, my dad asked my doctor about a little rash that had shown up on him.

I dismissed myself to the restroom. When I returned, they informed me that dad had been ushered out of the hospital and sent home to go back to their home to recover and I would be staying at the hospital until he returned.

He had been diagnosed with shingles, which was very contagious for any of the patients in the clinic who had no immune systems. The doctor wouldn't even let him stay on that floor with the other patients and walked him to the elevator and dad asked if he could tell me bye. The doctor said no, that he was so sorry. Dad had to go, but their prayers had been answered! Dad felt a little lost with nothing to do at first, but he did okay. He needed rest too. From that point forward, it was miracles after miracles. Seeing my blood count go higher, seeing my red blood cells grow. Less than five months from receiving the transplant, I saw them do something I had never seen before. They began removing iron from my body, as they would actually take blood from me in a similar way you give a blood donation.

My hemoglobin kept getting better and better and because of this, they would remove about a pint of blood a week to remove the iron instead of using any more chemicals. My body was healing. It was a long long journey. It involved some rocky points where they did not know what was happening to me. Everything had gone well, I was healthy had a fantastic immune system, but I began having other issues. I had been taken off the anti-depressants they required that I take when I began. There was always a regimen in place that they gave every patient when they began. Chemo is so hard on the body that it can cause other chemicals, hormones to be thrown off balance. They believed this anti-depressant worked to help offset what the chemo affected.

My sister had practically begged my doctor to take me off this particular anti-depressant because I was not myself.

Kristie told me what it was like trying to hold a conversation with me during that time. She said I barely finished sentences and would fall asleep while trying to talk and even drooled. However, things slowly changed. We did not know what was wrong. The first couple of weeks off the medicine I was fine, but then I would shake almost jerking sometimes, and I could not lower my arms to my sides. I began walking very very slowly and became extremely emotional. They were at their last straw as dad had been with me six months and had to at some point get back to his life with my mother. They did not know what else to do. They thought they were going to have me hospitalized! We literally were on that stage.

I met with my therapist again (also required regimen) and she began asking my dad certain questions and suddenly she jumped up and said I'll be right back. When she talked to the doctors, she explained that I was in a very very deep depression. That was the first time I understood depression could be chemically based. Before that time, I always thought it was spiritual or emotional only. This was new. She recommended a particular medication and the doctors agreed that they would give me 10 days and they would make the decision whether to bring me into the hospital. I was also told this medicine normally took 14 days to take effect. This medicine was an anti-depressant, but it only affected the serotonin level.

Day 2 after beginning this medicine I remember waking up and my thoughts felt clear. It was as though I suddenly began to feel normal and I remember being able to brush my teeth with just one hand where I had been using both hands as I would shake so badly. Day 3 as I woke up I knew everything was changed as I put my hands to my sides and walked across the room like normal. I quickly changed and bolted to dad's apartment, which was next door to mine and I knocked on the door. Dad opened and reminded me that he was going to come over soon. I said, "I needed to come in." As I walked in I looked at him and smiled and he was in shock. I walked across the room, sat down in the chair and said "Dad, I'm finally myself." The nurses cried and kept asking me to walk across the room for them at the clinic. When you go through something like this those that take care of you become very close to you, just as if you were family and they were so excited. I continued to get better and dad was able to return to my mom.

My dad and I have talked about this season and something that the Lord taught us both during this time. Many times, we say we believe the Lord and yet sit on pins and needles, timidly. We want to believe and even attempt to. We may even reach the point of believing and placing our faith in Jesus and then try to help Him figure things out and help Him accomplish something. What I experienced during that season in my life was not just believing Him, but also truly trusting Him and believing Him completely. I let go. I gave it to Him and let go. In order to go through this process I had to let go and trust the Lord to guide every step made, every decision made every moment that was encountered. There would be times that I had no strength in my body to walk or barely enough energy to take my shower and then get dressed. It would wear me out and I would have to rest after that. There was no strength in my arms at times to pick up the Bible and read. During this season, others read to me and many others that are dear friends would come and pray for me and spend time with me. I had to rest in God. It is the most amazing place to be and to stay, to remain there.

EIGHTEEN

This chapter was written by my parents to share their thankfulness and their testimony as a witness to God's faithfulness and love

A LOVE LETTER TO JESUS

Misty was a surprise baby born April 8, 1972. Gracie, her mom, was rushed to the hospital expecting to deliver one big boy and we were blessed with twin girls, God's gift to us. The dream I had about a little blond headed girl had come to pass. Misty only weighed 3 lbs. 11 oz. and had to stay in the hospital until she was up to 5 lbs. That ended up taking 6 weeks. Her beautiful sister, Kristie was a healthy 5 lbs. 4 oz. and went right home with Mom.

We were soon informed that Misty had several health problems. She had a heart defect and her red cell count was low. At just a few days old, she was given a 3 cc transfusion of her mom's blood in her little scalp. That's just what she needed, God provided.

Her blood count went back down and we were informed that she had a blood disorder that they were unable to diagnose. We were cautioned that we should prepare for the worst, that she might live only a short time.

That was Unacceptable.

At eleven months, Misty received another gift from God. A hematologist, diagnosed Misty with a very rare bone marrow disease named Diamond Black-Fan Anemia, known as DBA. The good news was that this hematologist was very familiar with this disorder and she immediately started Misty on steroids and "Praise God", Misty's system responded. The bad news was that most patients died at an early age, rarely older than a teenager.

There were some very difficult years and some really close calls. Misty was very prone to developing pneumonia which caused us to have to make two emergency trips to return Misty from Oklahoma to the hospital in Ft. Worth to an oxygen tent. She also developed severe asthma. Both were successfully treated and outgrown. Thank you Lord.

At 4 years old, Misty had heart surgery to correct a restricted aorta artery. That morning, an experimental Echo machine detected a second operable defect that made the operation successful. Thank you Lord.

Misty continued to be treated with steroids and an occasional blood transfusion, which kept the DBA in check for many years.

At the emotionally sensitive age of 12, Misty was fitted with a Milwaukee back brace to control the severe curvature taking place in her spine. She suffered the humiliation of it for 4 hard years until the curving stopped. Thank you Lord.

In 1993, the doctor s began to treat the DBA with an experimental drug, which worked for about two years and then quit. We were back to transfusions at about 6 week intervals. At least it allowed her body to get some momentary relief from the steroids.

In 1998, both Misty and Gracie saw a vision, which implied that God was curing Misty. Suddenly and miraculously, the

DBA went away and no treatment or medication was required for over two years. It had gone into remission.

In the year 1999, Misty moved to San Antonio, TX to continue her college education. Then in 2000, just as suddenly as it seemed to end, the DBA returned with a vengeance and transfusions were once again the answer to keeping Misty alive. God provided a new hematologist who immediately called the doctor who became her transplant doctor. He specialized in and taught stem cell transplantation around the world. Her hematologist called the institute that does transplants in Texas and made an appointment for Misty to see them. The doctor began the process of getting Misty scheduled for a stem cell transplant - one more miracle for Misty. The unheard of remission lasted just long enough for stem cell transplanting to become a reality. Praise God.

Before we began, we were assembled as a team and given a thorough run-down on what was expected of each person. We were informed that once started, there was no backing out. In addition, we were informed that there had been no successful attempts to cure DBA. I, dad, was the only family member available 24/7 for the next 5 months so I became Misty's designated caregiver and became solely responsible for Misty's welfare outside the clinic. This arrangement created an invaluable relationship between Misty and me. I've said that every father needs to go thru a process like this with a son or daughter. I compare the bond formed to that of a Mother and her baby. It is truly spiritual. Lord, we trust you.

The doctors first had to use chelation therapy to reduce Misty's excessive iron levels built up by transfusions. After 7 months of treatment without success, at the very last available day, overnight the levels suddenly dropped to normal, allowing the transplant to proceed on schedule. Thank you Lord. Now we need a matching stem cell donor.

Lab tests had determined that of all Misty's relatives, her sister Kristie was the only match, and not only a match, but a perfect match to be Misty's stem cell donor. In Jan 2003, Kristie came from Iowa and after several days of intense and painful preparation, her blood was drawn and sent through a centrifuge, which separated out the valuable stem cells. The cells were good and we had more than was required. The cells were then frozen and stored until Misty's system was fully prepared to receive them. Thank you Lord.

The beginning of the transplant process required Misty to enter the hospital for a 5-day long intense chemotherapy treatment, which over a few weeks' time, was to completely wipe out Misty's immune system.

Only hours, before Misty entered the hospital, we had a time of prayer in her apartment, believing that the Lord would oversee everything that took place during the entire transplant. Following the prayer time, the Lord gave Misty's mom a scripture for Misty to rely on during the transplant.

It was Isaiah 43:1-3 and it reads:

"But now, thus says the LORD, who created you, O Jacob, And He who formed you, O Israel: "Fear not, for I have redeemed you; I have called you by your name; You are Mine. When you pass through the waters, I will be with you; And through the rivers, they shall not overflow you. When you walk through the fire, you shall not be burned, nor shall the flame scorch you. For I am the LORD your God, The Holy One of Israel, your Savior;"

Her system was tested daily and the chemo worked exactly as planned, and by the way, Misty went through the chemo without getting sick, or having a headache or missing a single meal. Thank you Lord. We all learned a valuable lesson here on trusting the Lord and the scripture given Misty, fit her situation repeatedly during her recovery.

Other than the five days of chemo, all the rest of Misty's treatment and recovery was as an outpatient. Every day for the first 100 days, Misty and I got up early, ate breakfast and drove across San Antonio to check in at the clinic by 7 a.m. That was a real commitment.

On April 1, 2003, the medical team thawed out Kristie's stem cells and they were injected into a port placed in Misty's chest. That began a journey that changed all our lives. A new birthday for Misty, thank you Lord

On a regular basis, the doctor would bring us up to date on what the, almost daily, lab work would show to be taking place in Misty's body. Critical milestone dates were projected and without fail, these milestones were met and Misty's body was progressing at the precise rate anticipated.

By late August, Misty's body had fully accepted the new stem cells and her bone marrow, for the first time in her life, was producing new, healthy red blood cells. In fact there were so many cells that the lab had to draw blood to reduce the excessive number of red cells from Misty's system. <u>An overwhelming success</u>. <u>The first time that DBA had lost the battle and was defeated.</u>

Near the end of Misty's transplant recovery, her doctor told me that everything about Misty's transplant had been absolutely miraculous. I told him that we, as a family, believe that the entire thing, including his involvement, was a miracle from God. It was all in God's control and in His time.

Misty will soon be ten years out and has a totally new life, thanks to her Lord.

Misty, mom and dad at Thanksgiving 2012.

NINETEEN

STARTING DOWN A NEW ROAD

Within a year of the transplant, I began doing graphic design again on the side and took a lot of walks for exercise. I felt great. I had gone on a two-week trip where I had gotten sick before going and I had started retaining water or swelling in my ankles and feet. By the time I got back from this trip I was hospitalized for two weeks taking antibiotics by drip and getting well. I had to see a kidney specialist as they also found a blood clot in my kidneys. I was losing a lot of protein in the urine. I remember this doctor very carefully trying to explain to me that I had a kidney disease and there were three possible outcomes. Either the person had to have a kidney transplant, that they just dealt with this off and on all their life or it would just go away, but there "wasn't a cure." I laughed aloud so hard. He probably thought I had lost it.

That is not how everyone takes that news though I am sure. I had been told this kind of news more than one time in my life. I told him, it is the third option only, because you see doctor my God is bigger than that! He is my healer! "He has brought me from death to life and there isn't anything that He can't handle, and nothing you are going to share with me is going to shake that." Just watch as my God takes care of this and watch as He heals me. I want you to see who He is and you will see that He is greater. I told him not to worry, that he hadn't offended me. I asked him not to be so timid and to be more direct please.

I left that office waiting for miracles. I had to take practically bucket loads of potassium tablets. I had to take blood thinners because of the clot and I took Lasix to remove all the excess fluid that had built up because of the kidneys being in distress. Still, I watched and waited. When I moved from San Antonio about a year later I remember walking into that doctor's office and sitting in the room. He looked at me and just said, "Well Misty, you were right. It's gone. It is all gone." I just smiled and said, "See?" You can't deny Him. My God is so wonderful, such a loving Father! I have a new life now. Medicine free and thankful and praising my God continually! He answered my prayers, and in such a way that I never expected.

I moved from San Antonio and began a new life apart from an abusive marriage that I also was saved from at that time. Apart from the health issues, God saved me from a very painful and difficult place, which had been one of the hardest things I had walked through up to that time. While during the time of the transplant things had seemed better in the marriage, but shortly following that time, as I got stronger and healthier, there was so much more that surfaced than before and for the first time I was able to see what it really was. It was abuse and I had to get out. God put me on a new track. I sought the Lord for wisdom and direction continuously and when I was staying at my parent's house, I still remember a powerful dream I had. I had been asking the Lord what to do next and in this dream, I remember the Lord saying you will go when the light turns green as I was standing at a stop light in my dream. Suddenly it turned green and I stepped forward.

At that moment, I awoke and for the next five minutes or more, I saw a green light right in front of my face that I could not shake. It didn't leave me. I knew it was time to go forward. Eventually, making my way back up to Iowa to where my twin was and then on my own.

"**<u>Wait and listen</u>**, *everyone who is thirsty!* **Come** *to the waters; and he who has no money, come, buy and eat! Yes,* **come**, *buy [priceless, spiritual] wine and milk without money and without price [simply for the self-surrender that accepts the blessing].*

Why do you spend your money for that which is not bread, and your earnings for what does not satisfy? Hearken diligently to Me, and eat what is good, and let your soul delight itself in fatness [the profuseness of spiritual joy].

Incline your ear [submit and consent to the divine will] and **<u>come to Me</u>**; **hear**, *and* **your soul will revive**; *and I will make an everlasting covenant or league with you, even the sure mercy (kindness, goodwill, and compassion) promised to David."*

Isaiah 55

Take My yoke upon you and learn of Me, for I am gentle (meek) and humble (lowly) in heart, and you will find rest (relief and ease and refreshment and recreation and blessed quiet) for your souls.

Matthew 11:28-30

TWENTY

DIVINE INSTRUCTIONS

After this very difficult season in my life, I was not particularly interested in getting together with anyone at all. I was very happy being healthy, exercising and spending time with the Lord and making new friends. The Lord did eventually bring someone in my life, but I let him know right up front this was not going to be serious we were just friends.

Well, thankfully, he became more than a friend and we got married! He had a good paying job and so did I. We lived in Cedar Rapids, IA, where we met. It was beautiful and we enjoyed our lives. We were connected with a great church there, we went on vacations and spent time doing things we liked, but God was working on us. There is a desire the Lord put in our hearts and we wanted to help others who needed a place to stay. We thought it would be great to buy a small motel because we wanted to help homeless veterans and missionaries that were in from the mission field and needed rest.

Well, an opportunity arose and it was a very good deal. It included a guaranteed income for three years with contracts for construction workers that would ensure the revenue of the motel and that alone would pay off the debt of the motel. With this great opportunity staring at us, we jumped headfirst and put the house up for sale. Would it sound wrong to say that I believe the Lord messes with us sometimes? What I mean is we had to be pushed out of our comfort zones in order to go forward. Try to picture a potter working with clay, the Lord being the potter and we are the clay. There's a lot of work to make clay into something useable.

Our friend/real estate agent encouraged us that Monday not to be discouraged if it took a while for it to sell. After all, the market at that time was not great. We were excited about the prospect of the move and didn't think twice. On Thursday of that week was the recorded flood of Cedar Rapids, IA, in June of 2008. Our home was not touched, however much of Cedar Rapids was and that included our jobs which changed a bit, although we didn't lose either of them thankfully. Our friend/real estate agent called the day of the flood and said, "Whatever you're doing, whatever project you're in the middle of, finish it! I have people who want to see your house next week." It went that fast! Three weeks after being listed, it had a contract, the only one it got and it sold.

The following Monday, after the contract was in place, we decided to go see the property that we were going to purchase and tell them our good news. We wanted to work on the paperwork, and redo some things because banks were having a hard time giving us a loan for a place that didn't have a lot of paperwork to look at to ensure a loan. We tried that motel's own bank, and they were willing to talk with us. Our plan was to go up there on Monday and straighten things out, get things worked out on paper, re-sign things and get ready to go, as we would need to be moved in three weeks! We now had a deadline.

We were told that morning that the owner of the property on the previous Friday, the day we got the contract on the house, had decided to take a cash offer that was put on the table and run with it. It had sold and we could do nothing about it. We literally couldn't talk. I truly mean, no words would come out of our mouths for hours. I literally could not say anything. I felt numb. We both did. We had just sold a house and now we ourselves were going to be without a home. We thought about renting an apartment in the area and continuing to work our jobs, but with the flood that had taken place in the area, there were no apartments available at all.

There is a lot that transpired after this, but in effect, we began looking at other places we had originally seen in the beginning of our search. On one trip, I spotted a town that I was reminded of because of a conversation my sister and I had. The night I told her about our plans to move to Missouri and that we were leaving our jobs and buying a motel (our families thought we had lost our minds!), she said, "Have you ever heard of _____, Iowa? There is this person there that has a B&B and you should go see it, and by the way they go to my church." What did she not hear? I had just told her where we were moving, but she asked me questions instead. That conversation got lost somewhere in the recesses of my mind until that day.

As we were driving through this town, we looked around it and decided to call on this B & B the next day. It had no for sale signs outside, so I was not sure. There was a woman who answered and told me that both properties were for sale. Did she say two properties? We went to look at them. We could tell they needed some remodeling on the older portions, but it is amazing the things you sometimes miss! They said it was owner financing and we agreed this was it. It was a motel and a B&B.

On the day we moved in, which was two weeks later, I told Kristie thank you and that we would have never thought of it if she hadn't mentioned it on the phone that day. She looked at me so strangely and said that she never remembered telling me that information on the phone, and that she didn't even know this woman before we moved in. What? All I know is that I had heard her clearly that day and even my husband heard her!

Well, anyway, long story, it was so much work, so much joy and again, so much heartache. We have wonderful friends, Dwight and Anne Johnson that came and stayed and helped us through the winter and we spent awesome times with the Lord together. We had Bible Studies every week where we would spend time in the Lord's presence. It was awesome. It was usually after we had worked all day, barely had time to clean up and would just make it in time. Before spring, they had to go back down south with family, as they had to take care of their things too. Eventually, some problems arose with the financial side, and we had to walk away. Instead of keeping us in that difficult situation, the Lord brought us to a safe place.

We walked away from our home and business after a short time, just over a year and walking away with just our personal belongings. It's hard to fathom sometimes. Occasionally we still talk about it. We really enjoyed doing the breakfasts for others and ministering to them, serving them and we met so many great people.

I am reminded the Lord wants us to see. He wants us to see Him, to know Him, and to let go of the things of this world that we are holding to so tightly. Because He took us through this time, it has been like a stripping away, a cleansing if you will. It is because He loves so much and because He desires so much for us to be with Him and to know Him that He takes us through these hard places. If we yield to what He's doing, we will come closer to Him, rather than farther away. I'm thankful, so thankful for the times we had there and yet I'm even more thankful for the time since then as He's removed so many of the things we thought we had to have.

Abba,

When my gaze turns towards you and I realize how close you are. You are here with me. Everything else fades away. Nothing else matters. All my heart desires is to please you, to see you to dance with you, to worship you. I long for you and I know you long for me. You have placed this desire for you within me and it burns like a fire. Only you can satisfy me. You created me to fellowship with you, to be with you. You are not unreachable. You have not forsaken us. In fact, it's always been your desire for us to be with you. It is we who turn away. Please forgive me, please forgive us for focusing on me, on my, my, my, my. It is all about you Jesus… It is all about your Kingdom and your reign here in this earth. You desire for us to know who we are in you. In you, we are your family. That is huge! We are made your family Abba. Thank you for meeting with me and thank you for calling me, choosing me. Thank you for making me yours… I love you…

Know, recognize, and understand therefore that the Lord your God, He is God, the faithful God, Who keeps covenant and steadfast love and mercy with those who love Him and keep His commandments, to a thousand generations,

Deuteronomy 7:8-10

I love those who love me, and those who seek me early and diligently shall find me.

Proverbs 8:16-18

TWENTY-ONE

HE SAID TO COME
AWAY WITH HIM

It was necessary to tell you about the last season, where the business was no longer to tell you about this season, because this is the best part.

We have friends that gave us a place to stay when we left. We stayed in a 200-year-old house. That was an experience in itself. We had nothing income wise except for the graciousness of our friends. Al began work delivering pizza which helped as we would get the mishaps at the end of the night sometimes and this is much of what we ate, but I could not find any work myself in the small town we were staying in and we were sharing a car. It was tough, but oh the time that I spent alone with the Lord! I wouldn't trade it for anything. Imagine wall heaters in an old home with none in the bathroom. While in the fixing up stages of the house, I had fallen off a ladder into the bathtub while painting and landed on my tailbone. I don't know how I managed to get to the couch, which I couldn't sit on or lie down on. All I could do was begin to pray and ask the Lord to intervene. I know He did because I physically felt a change in my body, and I was then able to prop myself against the couch. With not being able to paint for a while, it was too cold to stay outside, no car to drive around in during the day, and trying to stay warm in at least one room was the only place I could go. I had no internet (usually), no television, no radio, and my cell phone was only working sometimes because of lack of funds.

Literally, I believe the Lord brought me to that moment, because I then had no distractions, no business, nothing. I'm learning all the distractions around us keep us from being able to hear Him, and keep our eyes and minds on other things. He is jealous over us the Word tells us and that we aren't to be consumed with things or "doing" things. He is much more interested in what we are becoming then in our doing. There are always things we can find to do, but this is often busy work. Jesus gave a very strong word to us when He said that He only did what He saw the Father doing and only said what He heard the Father say. The Word of God does say if you seek Him, you will find Him, when you seek Him with all your heart. When you set your "stuff" aside and all the distractions, making room for Him and putting Him first, He will meet you there. The best part is that we can come to know how great He really loves and it is because He desires so much to have a one on one relationship with us. He is the one that puts the desire within us to know Him. It wouldn't be there except for Him.

Arise [from the depression and prostration in which circumstances have kept you—rise to a new life]! Shine (be radiant with the glory of the Lord), for your light has come, and the glory of the Lord has risen upon you!

Isaiah 60:1-3

Therefore He says, Awake, O sleeper, and arise from the dead, and Christ shall shine (make day dawn) upon you and give you light.

Ephesians 5:13-15

Misty and Albert in the park, New Braunfels, TX.

EPILOGUE

This book began with a set of scriptures, Isaiah 55. The way that verse begins is a key, I believe. Wait and listen. We must make time, room for Him.

When I began asking the Lord *again* about writing this book, I was still asking him questions. I didn't know that there was a particular question still in my heart and I thought it had been dealt with long ago. I only knew it was there when the Lord gave me the answer. The question I still had in my heart was why. Why all these things Lord? As I mentioned at the beginning of this book, He showed me that I am, that we are His love letters to share Christ, give Christ. We must know Him, because He loves so much this is His plan and His plan is awesome.

The seventh angel then blew [his] trumpet, and there were mighty voices in heaven, shouting, The dominion (kingdom, sovereignty, rule) of the world has now come into the possession and become the kingdom of our Lord and of His Christ (the Messiah), and He shall reign forever and ever (for the eternities of the eternities)! Revelation 11:15

That's right, the Kingdom of God reigning in all the earth and the Heavens! The Word says that God will create a new Heaven and a new earth and that the righteous shall inherit the earth. Those that overcome will reign with Christ. The Word also talks about the things that will happen in the earth, not like the Mayan calendar that everyone talks about suggesting everything coming to an end, but yes all things that don't exalt God and are raised up against Him or are praised or worshiped by man that are outside of the Lord will all come to nothing. He is a Holy God and He formed all that exists with his very Word. This awesome and Holy God wanted our relationship with Him restored with Him adopting us as His children and restoring what was lost in the garden of Eden. He has given us the opportunity to choose once again to partake of His Son, Christ Jesus, the Tree of Life, which was restored to us. We have the opportunity to have abundant eternal life or be eternally separated from Him. I want life and I want to reign with Him! How awesome! There are many that we hear saying everything is fine and everything is going to go your way. Well, as we hear the Lord and we respond to His voice He makes the changes in us that we cannot. He transforms us. The closer we become to Him and the more acquainted we are with Him, the less we desire things of the world. He changes what we see and how we see and He changes the desires of our hearts as we begin desiring Him above all others and all things. We also begin to see the things that the Lord is dealing within us, the things that must go so He alone can reign in our hearts.

It begins first with coming to Him. Remember the wait and listen part? Well, He also says numerous times, come to me. We must come and respond. That first purpose we are given is to have a relationship with him, a gift that's been given to us. That relationship is restored because of Jesus.

In order to know Him personally you have to go straight to the Source! He teaches us through His Word, through speaking to our hearts and He does speak through others for our benefit too, but the more we come to Him, the more we know His voice and the more we know Him. You know what? Everything we are and everything we do is to begin right there first. We must have that relationship and everything else becomes clear when that happens. He makes it clear, as we can't do that. He does it. Oh, that we would really know that it really is all about just that one thing and everything else begins to make sense from there. He sets us free from confusion and darkness. He saves us from an empty existence without Him. When you feel that pull in your heart and you think about Him. He's speaking to your heart. Right there He made you aware of Himself. He wants to spend time with YOU and wants you to know Him.

When we come to Him, simply waiting upon Him quietly, He will meet us there. This is that beginning of coming to know Him, and having a relationship with Him. We can't know someone that we don't spend time with. We were created for Him, and to glorify Him and as we get to know Him personally, this love that He has transforms us. Instead of asking what's in it for me, our hearts will melt in His presence as we experience a love that is indescribable.

But the Comforter (Counselor, Helper, Intercessor, Advocate, Strengthener, Standby), the Holy Spirit, Whom the Father will send in My name [in My place, to represent Me and act on My behalf], He will teach you all things. And He will cause you to recall (will remind you of, bring to your remembrance) everything I have told you.

John 14:25-27

He gives us a new mind, the mind of Christ and transforms

our entire being. We must continue to meet with Him to know Him and learn from the Lord.

The enemy of our souls has enjoyed far too long twisting this to look like something it is not. Man has come to believe that he must earn his way to the Lord, do better and better and keep everything just right. We cannot. He made it a gift that we can't earn. He made it possible for us to be with Him once again and we must choose this life.

His very design from the beginning:

"May blessing (praise, laudation, and eulogy) be to the God and Father of our Lord Jesus Christ (the Messiah) Who has blessed us in Christ with every spiritual (given by the Holy Spirit) blessing in the heavenly realm!

Even as [in His love] He chose us [actually picked us out for Himself as His own] in Christ before the foundation of the world, that we should be holy (consecrated and set apart for Him) and blameless in His sight, even above reproach, before Him in love.

For He foreordained us (destined us, planned in love for us) to be adopted (revealed) as His own children through Jesus Christ, in accordance with the purpose of His will [because it pleased Him and was His kind intent]"

Ephesians 1:3-5

Some may be reading this and thinking well, all of this is true, but I'm already there. I got it or, you're really preaching to the choir. As long as we have bits and pieces of our lives mixed in with, what the world says is good and parts of that mixed in what the Lord desires, there is "mixture." The Lord is clear that if we are a friend of the world, we are an enemy of God. We cannot resemble the world either. Christ must literally be living in and through us.

But the day of the Lord will come like a thief, and then the heavens will vanish (pass away) with a thunderous crash, and the [material] elements [of the universe] will be dissolved with fire, and the earth and the works that are upon it will be burned up.

Since all these things are thus in the process of being dissolved, what kind of person ought [each of] you to be [in the meanwhile] in consecrated and holy behavior and devout and godly qualities,"

2 Peter 3:10-11

The Kingdom of God here in us – with us – and becoming more and more visible. To the world, it looks darker and dimmer and it will continue to growing increasingly more. My God, you have secured me, created me from before there was time. The bride you are cleaning her up, bringing her together, all of the parts of her growing closer to you, becoming one with you. Jesus...your bride yearns for you. I yearn for you.

There are times that my vision stays shifted heavenward and focused on the Spirit. I know you are drawing me and your eye is focused upon me. You have captured me. You are my love. You have shown me and continue to hide me in you. There is much you desire to reveal of yourself and I desire to know all of you. You have placed the longing in my heart for you. Only you can satisfy. You alone are worthy and Holy. You are worthy and full of Glory. Your glory fills the temple. We are your temple, your living temple. We have been qualified yet we did not earn it. You have lifted the burdens that weigh down. Your burden is light and your yoke is easy. You didn't just say it. It's true. When I take something upon myself that you did not give me, it's very heavy. Your peace fills us your light overwhelms us and wraps us. Your fire burns until only you remain within us. Your fire, your Holy fire removes all that cannot glorify you, all that doesn't resemble you. Fill us with your song and your dance. You gave us your power and authority in Jesus. Flow through us and from us that others will come to the brightness of your rising up within us.

I see myself standing before the clouds and speaking for them to calm and they do. I see bright and beautiful colors of trees, flowers and buildings that are created and fashioned by you for us to enjoy... to enjoy with you.

I see the enemy scatter and fall. I see you remain and fill all things as you have filled all things with yourself. Exciting these days we are in, that we will walk in your Spirit as one body, Your body, and with one heart, Your heart, one Spirit, Your Spirit, glorifying You!!

I see walking hand in hand with you Jesus on sandy beaches,

dancing in Your Light, laughing and dancing and reigning with You, worshiping You, loving You, loving You Father, remaining in you. What is so amazing is this love You place in us, is the love You have for us and You are that, love. You fill us with Yourself. This love You put in us is the reason we can love. Without You, we are empty.

All that remains can only come from you. My inheritance begins now and has already begun. Eternity has already begun!

You have said that You are not a respecter of persons and that all that will may come to You. When we believe you and we come to You and we repent from our doing our own ways and that dead place of sin, You want us to know that we are now made Your family. We have inheritance with Christ. What a privilege to know You and remain with You forever.

ABOUT THE AUTHOR

Misty Lea Chladek received her associate's degree studying graphic design, continuing education in photojournalism and anthropology. Misty's had her artwork in a few galleries and enjoyed serving guests while they operated a B & B in Iowa. Currently, she is an online transcriptionist and lives with her husband in southwestern Missouri.